NEW CONTEXTS: 5

𝑏

First published in paperback and ebook
format by **Coverstory** *books*, 2023

ISBN 978-1-7393569-2-7 (paperback)
ISBN 978-1-7393569-3-4 (eBook)

www.coverstorybooks.com

NEW CONTEXTS: 5

Coverstory books

Table of Contents

Foreword

Whenever I pull together an anthology such as this, I am inevitably struck by the quality and variety of both the fiction and poetry being written today. Curating an anthology such as this is therefore both a joy and a challenge; after all, it is not easy to distil a couple of hundred pieces down into a manageable number to form a collection (in the present case, seventy-four pieces).

However, for this edition of *New Contexts* I was struck more than ever by the notion that the contributors had important things to say — and about significant topics too: war, disease, aging, love, refugees, our place in the world. These are all 'big' topics of course, and as such hardly novel; writers have been devoting their talents to addressing them for hundreds of years. Yet it struck me that many of the submissions for this book attempted to tackle their themes with a common sense of urgency.

Perhaps this is a reflection of our times; or perhaps it was merely my interpretation of them. Whichever is true, I am confident that *New Contexts: 5* represents another meritorious addition to our canon.

I hope you enjoy it.

Ian Gouge, August 2023.

Two and Six

Too perfectly round for a pebble,
almost hidden in the new-cut grass:
an old half crown. King George V,
1936 FID DEF IMP IND,
a fine old boy with a beard.

And back I flashed to a sixties day
and the garden fête. Remember those?
And if you don't, I'll understand.
But they were a cornucopia of fun
and there were riches in my hand:
half a whole crown for spending on
whatever, whatever that came the way
of my twelve-year-old self,
whose half a crown
wasn't there.
Just a sudden empty pocket.
A stoic refusal to blub.

The day, and the loss, as clear as glass
vases among the books and the tat.
My half crown, back in my pocket at last.
Once a fortune. Now a curio,
and barely even that.

Edward Alport

Resurrection Song

Resurrection Song
Nothing to see here today
says the hanging branch
as it dips its tip to the surface
like a point duty policeman,
waving the stream on its way.

No, not true at all,
there is so much to see:
a current augmented
by late melting snow,
levels that rise and fall;

frog spawn splayed in a puddle
by the riverside path,
clouds of black-eyed jellies
may never reach the tadpole stage,
emergent sunshine, pond is dried;

hyperactive, barrel-chest
white breast, dressed for dinner,
a water ouzel bounces, trills
as his statuesque prospective mate
quietly observes those diving skills;

wheeling buzzards squeal
delight from thermal height,
contrast, the lift and updraft slap
as pigeon wings flap
in a scrappy mating flight;

even crow is finding voice
from a monumental cross
in adjacent Victorian boneyard,
his singular plaintive baritone
addressed to his other half;

clustered around the hill top
hazel catkins hang
dew-dropping damp and limp
like forgotten socks
on a washing line;

whilst framed by ancient yews
the squat church tower pushes
parapet through the clinging mist
silenced like the peaceful sound
of eternity in hallowed ground.

Phil Askham

Red-Haired Red-Iron Woman

She wrestled with the legs of the
ironing table as she set it up in the
kitchen, beside hearth top dressed
with sea-salt jars, pepper grinders, olive oil
decanters brought by her snappers from distant
weather where peaches, grapes and figs ripen.
Cows munching curiously over moon hugging hedges,
she took clothes off the branches in a basket of wicker,
happy with their dawn-clinging dampness.
Fire-hot iron marches up seams and down pleats
singing sharp C's as she folds and flattens black-sheep
wool, linen, and muslin to slip in lavender niche.
The only bum note, the only wrinkle was husband me,
scorched and slain in a full-moon, red-iron fury.

John Atkinson

Sideshow

step right up, hurry, hurry,
before the show begins, my friends

that was a song she hadn't heard in ages, coming from a radio somewhere behind the horizontally striped windbreak.

She loved that song. Barefoot, sandals in one hand and Tim's proffered hand in the other, she sprang nimbly over a sandcastle, landing lightly with the grace of a dancer on the other side.

step right up, honey, honey, she sang and laughed her beautiful laugh, her fine blond hair catching in the late afternoon sun like a meteor shower, at least that's how Tim recorded it in his black notebook later that evening, alone in his room in the holiday cottage.

It's not 'honey, honey' he'd laughed, *its 'hurry, hurry';* it seemed even more urgent to him as he said it.

She'd said she'd done ballet as a child, like his mother; how she'd love her, he thought.

So graceful her poise, that fine head on a slim neck, held high. He'd watched with his heart in his throat as she'd danced on the edge of the surf, spinning complete circles and every bit of her so fine, fine arms pointing fine fingers, fine legs, fine ankles with fine arched feet pointing those slim fine toes; one day he would caress each digit, lovingly, slowly and capture the individual persona of all twenty in the beauty of his teenage verse.

He'd felt himself a lump beside her, his footsteps heavy in the sand where hers seemed to leave only the slightest of imprints; she touched the ground lightly, more airborne than earth connected.

He'd felt stupid standing there with his muscles, huge arms, chest, legs, six pack. It was true they brought him many admiring looks along the beach with her at his side and even a whistle or two from a group of shy teenage girls, but now he wondered suddenly what they were all for, he wasn't a lumberjack or scaffolder after all. He wondered how he'd suddenly changed from his small slim physique of old. Where had that light, quick, scrum-half had gone to, replaced one season to the next by a front row forward.

He adored her he'd decided, she was the 'one'. He'd revisit his A level Elizabethan poets with a new eye.

You're alright, she'd replied, laughing to the question he'd asked when he could finally no longer resist.

He was nice looking and a bit of holiday attention was no bad thing after all, she'd thought to herself. Someone to listen to her constant chatter, to hear her memories of this place, the family holidays of years past when her dear Dad was still alive, the caravan parked up in the farmer's field, over there. He didn't say much but that was up to him. He wrote in a little book now and then with a pencil and glanced up at her as if he would have liked her to ask him what it was he was writing, but she never had.

She certainly wouldn't have wanted an 'adorer' if he'd let that slip. No, their black Labrador was one 'adorer' enough, forever following her around with great longing eyes; certainly she wouldn't want a boyfriend like that, but who was talking about boyfriends anyhow? She didn't really see what all the fuss was about.

Evening washed further over the hot day's beach and with it people packed up and left, taking tents, rugs, picnics, inflatables, windbreaks, kites, towels, bags and more with them. The sand strewn parking lot began to empty and the ice cream shack was shuttered up and orange in the low sun which had burst out beneath the cloud, 'that guileful sun had slipped the guards' grey hands and burst with all its' full, piercing urgency into his heart'.. he'd written that later in bed, his parents still downstairs, their voices low, the words not fully recognizable and he'd put the book under the bed before turning out the light, thinking of her.

She and Tim said their goodbyes, quite formally it seemed to her. She put out her slim hand to his extended one, laughing as she did.

'Au revoir' she'd said. She thought there were some things he might have wanted to say but she skipped away whilst it seemed he was still composing them behind his sombre-looking face.

'I'll write' he called after her, the words hanging momentarily in the air as if demanding a response. She waved a hand above her head, not turning and she grew smaller as he looked after her with eyes more full of longing than her Labrador, she still barefoot on the sandy tarmac path, her sandals still in her hand. He treasured the fact that she had said 'au revoir' and not goodbye, that, at least, was something to hold onto.

At the youth hostel she met up again with Dianne, who apologized for leaving her alone, having wanted to spend the day with Dan whom she'd met at the arcade the evening before. By the afternoon it was clear that Dianne was bored with him and he with her. She'd been back at the hostel by four, reading her copy of 'Women in Love'. Julie didn't tell her about Tim, she realized that as Dianne began to question her about her day, that it wasn't necessary, important.

The flood tide pushed its unstoppable way up that sun-warmed beach, it smoothed away all the marks left by visitors to the beach that day. It smoothed away the holes the children had dug as defenses against the sea, it washed away the sandcastles, the small windbreak holes, the paw marks, the footprints, the hopscotch tracks, the volleyball, cricket, football pitches. It washed away the half-eaten sandy sandwich, the ice cream sticks, the forgotten paper cup, the red leather bookmark with Wells Cathedral on it. It washed away the stone circles, the shell circles, the faces made of shells, the words scratched in the sand, 'Rick', 'Michael,' 'I hate my bruver'.

In the dark when a red light flashed somewhere out on the sea four times slowly and then stopped for a moment before repeating the same mournful sequence, when the sky was pillowy black and looked as if it held gallons of rain and yet the air was still warm and close, the tide reached its height on that beach and washed away a heart scratched in the sand with a stick, an arrow diagonally through it and on one side the name 'Tim' and on the other 'Julie'.

The first holidaymakers arrived on the beach before nine am, for it was a Saturday and would no doubt be busy, being another glorious day, another 'scorcher' as the headlines read. The beach was huge, the sea a distant beautiful blue with a thin straight line of white surf from left to right where it ended each side in small rocky cliffs, topped with grass where small figures with hats could already be seen walking, stopping now and then for half seen dogs to rejoin them. The beach was a brand-new canvas, flat and wide without a single mark as that first family from Birmingham walked across it, feeling like they were the first and only ones stepping out onto a virgin desert island. A few white shells here and there, a few stones, but nothing with any pattern left by others. 'Go on, write on me', the blank page seemed to say, today is your day, make your marks, write your words, what it didn't mention was that later today, not so long from now, they too would all be gone.

Two girls sat on the squashy seat of a train carriage, opposite each other. They didn't speak, they were happy to be looking out at the coast along which they were travelling, they were lucky that the window was on the right side for that. It was a bit hot there in the sun but worth it and they had the sliding window as far up as it would go. The sea was flat, the sky without a cloud. Here and there a small colored boat, fishing perhaps. Further out two white sails. An estuary mouth with sailing boats sitting in mud, some at an angle, others vertical on two uprights below their white muddied bellies. 'Blue Magic', she read on one, sitting closer to the sea-grassed sand. Over there a headland with a small town shimmering behind a hazy wall of heat.

The girls were on their way home, Dianne to her parents and her friend, Julie, to her mum. Julie craned her neck, that must be 'her' beach she thought; if she had been able to see all those miles, she would have seen a boy writing a postcard, sitting on that same beach. ' Our beach' he'd written on it simply, and underneath 'Au Re-voir, until we meet again, Tim'. He'd added what looked as if it might once had been a heart but had been amended to become a dragon's eye, a Welsh dragon's eye. He'd written her address in Stafford, not a part of the country he knew anything about and indeed his father would have said who would want to, but he wasn't his father as he kept telling himself. He'd forgotten to ask her surname so had simply written 'Julie' on the first line. It had set him contemplating what that surname might be; Matthews, Lawrence, what sort of names did people have 'up North' he wondered. He'd stuck on a small grey stamp with a youthful queen's head on it and a white dragon in the top left-hand corner. He'd run his tongue over its rear side and had thought of his saliva travelling by train and van and eventually entering her house, landing on a mat inside the front door to a house he had only vague images of. His kiss would be on that card as she picked it up, pinned it to her cork board in her small room at the back of the house overlooking a neat well-tended garden full of flowers.

That song came into Julie's head again. It was what the Germans would call an 'Ohrwurm', ear worm, she'd heard her German exchange student, Gretel, use that word when they'd been talking about a Michael Jackson song in her room; the tune was lodged there and wasn't going anywhere soon. She sang it to herself in her head, smiling.

Step right up honey, honey, before the show begins, my friends

Stand in line, get your ticket, I hope you will attend

She didn't know any other words, so she just hummed the tune to herself, over and over.

If she had known the other lines she might have sung on further:

See the man who's been cryin' for a million years, so many tears (so many tears)

See the girl who's collected broken hearts for souvenirs

It's more exciting than a one-man band

The saddest little show in all the land

So let the side show begin (hurry, hurry)

Hurry, hurry, step right up on in

Can't afford to pass it by

Guaranteed to make you cry

Alex Barry

"Sideshow" was a song recorded by American R&B soul vocal quintet Blue Magic, released in 1974. It was first released on the album *Blue Magic* and when issued as a single it sold over a million copies, going to No.1 R&B in April 1974 and No.8 pop in the United States in that summer. - Wikipedia

The Elms

It was the photograph that caused it,
a sudden heave of the chest,
a sensation such as a missing limb must give,
its absence still capable of causing pain.
The Shell Guide to Oxfordshire, by John Piper, 1951,
the black and white images carefully composed,
as was the fashion in those slow days.
And here, my own dear village, Shilton,
with Norman church and font,
the steep hill, the quiet pond.
The selected one shows the lazy back hill,
taken from high, an English summer's day,
under towering cumuli of dazzling white and myriad grey.
The elderflower, blinding with joy,
the cool dark shadows on a carless road.
A young mother holds a large sprung hooded pram against the slope.
Time and sun and heat and peace shimmer in a world gone by
and in the distance, their height increased by a grassed bank,
the silent giants stand,
guardians of the ancient village,
rook inhabited, stately sentinels,
their trunks gnarled and rough,
the great elms reach out huge arms to their dead selves,
burned forever upon my retina.

Alex Barry

Livid

Worst is the silence
clenched jaw bite-back
some lifetimes in its making

and whose dull chisel gouged this mark
what rusted wire   baling language
in its wake   words like love
seething quietly in the trash heap
  no soft places in this heart

as if every vessel
was meant to be broken
every tragedy left unfolded
you're made in this image
made for the mangling
made for the long path
  circling   as if pain
is the only option

its crooking finger signals you
          time to be those friends
come play in the badger hole
we'll show you a thing
you won't forget.

Clare Bercot Zwerling

Flower Vendor

The end of a long hot day under Mexican sun. We sit in evening cool in Oaxaca, drink icy Margaritas, eat tacos and enchiladas. Mariachis serenade diners. Peasant women, rebozos bright as the bougainvillea around the square, move between tables selling gaudy pots, silver jewellery. We have to turn them away. Students, limited money, limited luggage. Out of the shadows a child appears, weighed down by a basket brim-full with gardenias. She's beautiful. Simple handwoven dress hanging from her slight body. The air fills with heady perfume. Dark eyes smiling, she offers a single stem to each of us. We scrabble for pesetas.

Margaret Beston

A fine place to die

On the red planet a great storm has kicked
up dust-devils and blotted out the sun.
The fifteen-year-old rover sends out one
last message with its circuits' final spark:
My battery is low. It's getting dark.

Ama Bolton

Stranger

A white-hot sabre tallies a halogen gash across the cherry-red vibrancy of a gleaming hot-rod. The sun, penetrating the display window, brazenly fingers the smooth hood of a Ferrari F40. Outside, kids goggle, faces and hands marring the newly-washed glass. They linger for a while, but disperse at the approach of an adult. As if for their very lives, they scatter like a shoal of mackerel parting for the foreboding bulk of an ocean minesweeper. Collectively, they flee, as if from the approach of an unfed predator.

Leonard voices to the children that they are welcome. He calls out to invite them back. His words echo, unanswered, in the vacancy of early morning. Down the street, the youth have already fled.

Outside his door, he fidgets with an unwieldy set of keys, a hydra's head of choices, and opens the secret passage into a pirate's hideaway grotto, a dragon's lair full of rare goods and secondhand treasure. Together, he and the mid-August heat enter a cluttered space filled with endless wonders, the cramped quarters of a modest shop of curios and old collectibles.

For hours, one could hear a pin drop, the beating of one's heart, the vacancy of silence filled only by the musty aroma of old, yellowed pages, perhaps the occasional sigh.

Then, a soft note from a cherub on the wing. "Can we get one, Dad?" Leonard overhears from outside the open door. He shuffles among the crowded, stacked items, turning to observe a face of wide-eyed wonder, a glowing expression free from embellishment. Hovering close to the shopfront, an eager child's shadow stretches across a field of neatly displayed Hot Wheels. By the dozens, the toy cars shimmer like cut gems, precious baubles. Sparkling in the sunlight, they call to the neighborhood kids as if sirens singing out to passing sailors.

As he pretends to dust off some worn-edged, worm-eaten books, Leonard's peripherals devour the approaching steps of a could-be-customer. Through the door, a child tugs at his father's arm, the stubborn deadweight of an anchor impeding an outbound vessel. Clinging at his sleeve, a young boy averts the intended path of his stony-faced father. As if a gale, a stiff, shoreward wind, the little kid plants his feet, leans inward, an adamant assertion that a ship forgoes embarking from an island known for its buried treasure.

"How much for the car?" the father asks as he enters the crowded, little shop.

"Which one?" Leonard feigns ignorance to that which he already knows.

"Which one, Bud?" the man asks the boy who clutches to his side.

"The fast one! The red one!" At the end of an extended, skinny arm, a little finger points at the vague proximity of the Ferrari F40, dozens of other hot-rods beside it, many of them red.

The father frowns, studying the rainbow array of miniaturized speedsters, puzzling out the target to his son's inadequate description. Off to the side, Leonard smiles. He is fluent in enthusiasm. He does not puzzle out anything. He simply knows.

"Is this the one you're after?" He plucks up the F40 which is hot to the touch, a red ember, charged by the summer sun.

The child nods, fails to hide his wide, ecstatic smile. Slowly, unsure, his tentative nature wrestles with his over-excitement as he halfway commits to taking up the small car.

"Go on," Leonard urges the boy. "It's yours." The kid extends his hand and accepts the offered treasure. Holding it in his small, sweaty fingers, he beams with unfiltered joy, an honest emotion neither spoiled nor diluted by adulthood. He radiates as luminous as the sun that threatens to further bleach the spines of exposed, faded books all around him. In the purest form of delight, the boy shines as bright as the trinket he now possesses for himself, the fastest car in the neighborhood, perhaps the whole of the world.

"How much for the car?" the father asks again, unsmiling as he eyeballs Leonard.

"Consider it a gift," Leonard grins, sincere as a child.

"We don't take gifts from strangers," the child says, subdued, grieved by his own line in a well-rehearsed script.

"That's right," mutters the father, hands on hips. "How much?"

Leonard frowns, robbed of his gleeful moment. "Let's settle on a dollar," he says soberly, little more than a whisper. Without joy, he accepts the folded bill.

A father and son depart out into the heat of mid-August. A moment later, Leonard is once again alone. Among a myriad of trinkets, a cache of wondrous goods, he stands still, as if one of his countless curios. Little toy cars sparkle in the sun. In tidy rows they gleam, gorgeous and sleek. They call out, like sirens, but no one seems to hear.

James Callan

Little Clay Head

I formed you out of clay,
pushed my fingers into the malleable earth
of your body, finding the shape of you
in how your eventual being
succumbed to the pressure of my presses.

Your cranium in my palm,
the heat of my hands
smoothed your facial structure.
Without bones, I gave you my blood
in the pulse of each fingertip stroke.

No tools, aside from a small twig
selected from a cluster
of dried leaves on the ground.
I pushed it - one by one
into the sockets of your eyes,

finding all directions of a compass,
the degrees of a magic circle
into which I poured your lack of sight.
Like an ankh, I forced this magic wand
into your mouth, parting nonexistent lips.

I hold you in my hand. Behold the work
of my creation. You look so surprised,
perturbed, as if the merest semblance
of existence is enough to make you
stare wide-eyed and gasping. C'est la vie.

Joseph Chaplain

Mi Fathas boots

A lost mi Fatha owar ten year sin
An mi owd Hoggs wer warein thin

Ad kept Fathas owd Hogg boots
Thi tek mi back t mi roots

A kept em cos thi wert same size as mine
An a thowt wi sum work thid cum up fine

Thid bin int cuburd sin 2000 n 3
An a wer banna see ow thid fit mi

But the'd dreed out, n gon reet ard
Bein a farmer a weren't banna cob em int yard

Wi olass wore Hoggs wen it wernt t wet
Darned gud fur workin n walkin, best tha can get

Sum neets ad clean em
Wen thi wer dry, on t paper on me kne

Th'owd toothbrush scrubbin
Then blather em i Dubbin

Dark evy leather aw stitched triple er duble
T keep thi feet out o truble

Gud evy sole wi loadsa grip
Dizined like a knobbly snow tyre – no slip

Thi last wen tha gis em some jip
Wen a wer a teen a did t Pennine Way

We walked near tweny mile a day
Two undred n seventy mile in a fortneet

Mi Hoggs stood mi good, fre morning til neet
N the wer nobut me wi no blisters on mi feet

Anyow, mi owd-fellas boots wer a mess
So a gend up ont net thal gess

A wurkt stiff lether ard wi mi ands
An Neets Foot oil browt em t life

Wi gud black leather laces stuck in
Now a cun geet some rough rocky places

Feet comfy gud n dry, thi look reet well
N am chuffed, apun tha cun tell

A cud nair fill mi fathas boots tha see
Bur is owd Hoggs r still goin strong, n that'll d me.

Andrew Collinson

always the victim

saw your sister
at work the other night,
and i don't think she
recognized me;

i was hoping she wouldn't —

didn't want her to report
to you because then
i knew i might see your face
again,

but these years without you
have been some of the best i have
ever known —

when there are no weeds to pull
out the nutrients from all of
your flowers,
it gives you a chance to truly grow;

and i couldn't stomach another
conversation with you —

always the victim, even when you weren't;
really playing into that damsel in distress
trope and it made me wonder if anything
you ever told me was true.

Linda M. Crate

Oak Tree

The heel and sink of a shovel into soil that spring
to plant a cracked seed I held in one hand

like a wren's egg. A husk eager to split
and grow in the soak of leaves –

composted stories buried beneath my feet.
In darkness I said your name over –

starting with O and ending with a season
of sudden snow charming northern air.

How easily you balance sun and moons now
on your bare shoulders, how you load July air

with sweetness and shade. How bark grows rough
with age. Guardian of forget-me-nots, windflowers

bring me the spring of nesting song-thrush, the chime
of children playing long after bedtime.

Kerry Darbishire

Snow Tracks

Sudden snow
   reveals night traffic
     the un-shy language

of hunger above
   and below our feet: deer

fox   a stray cat   the rush
   of arrows stalled
     in the lawn like the weft

of a willow basket   voices
   muted

like lambs murdered
   by the fist of a drift
     this spotted flycatcher

frozen in my hand

Kerry Darbishire

Hesitation is Good

As long as we get our timing right,
as in the 'Hesitation Waltz' or that

moment in a tango when the audience
or maybe even your dance partner

starts to wonder if you are about
to go too far, to make a move

the pair of you have not rehearsed
because one or both believed it was

not possible, and suddenly you are
about to mime a scene straight out

of a barrio bar in Buenos Aires,
one of you will wind up slumped

over a table, and nobody can agree
what happened or who is in the wrong,

but maybe that moment will pass,
you will snap back into the rhythm,

and the audience will throw admiring
glances, or even applaud if the etiquette

of the venue allows it, and you will walk
off the dance floor, heads held high.

Brian Docherty

Waiting Area

Quiet like peace, space like silence.
A sleek black dream machine stands
road-ready in the corner.
A man, fish-like, noses round it,
a salesman watches, patient as any angler.
The coffee is good - and it's free.
I assume someone's delving, prying,
checking, changing; my prepaid service.

Somewhere, there is music,
somewhere, the patter of speech;
outside the sun is shining.
I take up my book and time,
like a trail, heads off into the distance.
I read until this phrase catches my mind:
'the frolic of the early marriage bed'.
It arrests me. I am suddenly gone.

Us, there, back then, our meetings,
our blood hot with desire.
'Frolic' I think, 'yes, it was like that...
wherever we were, it was always like that'.
I'm paging through memories
when the receptionist suddenly appears
with my car keys, smiling,
thinking she's doing the right thing.

Philip Dunkerley

Run Mum Run

At Brent Cross Mum talks in a loud voice — *look at this, look at that* — touching stuff. I try hard to ignore her. Half of 7R are there. I could die. I'm the only one with their mother. She has on that same puffa jacket, no make-up, her bushy hair all over the place, streaked with grey, and she's wearing her second best lace up geriatrics.

A few years ago there was still some hope for her. Just a *small* effort — a few nice jackets, silk tops, decent shoes, tights... But would she listen to us? Tights, she says, should only be used to hang apples in. You cannot breathe in them. As for high heels... They're the Western equivalent of Chinese foot binding torture. People (*men people*) must accept you the way you are. You are not there for their sexual gratification. Underwired? "We gave up wearing bra's decades ago, she boasts, "just so silly girls can go wiring themselves up again. Now the advertisers have got hold of you, Marks and *Spensive* has been reborn!" At this point she usually chokes herself laughing.

"Leggins," she goes on, "are the best garment ever invented. They have defeated the style fascists. They created a monster. What d'you see women wearing on the streets, at the school gates, tarted up with a little black top at parties, I ask you... Have you seen anyone wearing a garment inspired by Vivienne West-her-face, lately? Leggins! You wear them. I wear them. Gran wears them. Alice's new baby wears them. They fit nicely over your lumps and bumps — a thigh length top. Voila! Seamless from birth unto the grave. The only truly democratic garment ever invented..."

At BC, she swans over to the ponsy perfume counter to have a sneaky go at Opium — like her sister, Aunt Beth from Bath. Otherwise known as the buck stops here. "No!" I shout. "Don't!" "Don't worree, honey," she whispers. The snooty blond, very made-up beauty lady, looks down her nose at mum and says, pointing with two hands together, long red nails, "this side is the ladies, and this side is the men's," in a kind of Essex-cum-Selfridges accent. She must set the trap at nine in the morning and lay in wait for a whole new line of mums. Only I look around, my cheeks burning, and there are no other mums. Just mine. And neatly dressed, *normal* looking women, who look like they know what they're doing, and lean shop girls in crisp white blouses — and *half* of 7R. If the escalator could have swallowed me up... I see a group of my friends. "Don't talk," I order her "just don't talk." And I walk ahead of her... sheepishly.

"We'll go for tea," she says, pulling me towards the caff, or the Café de la Mer, as it prefers it to be called, though where la mer is on the north circular...

At school we call it, "La Mared". She gets two sandwiches, one cheese and tom, and one egg mayo. "We'll share" she says, just like she did when I was *eight*. And an extra cup in case I want a sip. I *want* a coke," I demand. "It's bad for you," she says. "It'll give you spots. It has nine spoons of sugar in it... or is it twenty? And a lot more besides." "Du know, when they gave it to hamsters... the hamsters ran frantically round for several minutes, then dropped dead. Poor little sods." We go and sit down. I feel my cheeks getting redder. "Take your sweater off," she says. "It's always so hot in here." My cheek accidentally brushes against her puffa jacket, and it feels all soft and silky, and for a moment I feel like I did when I was small, and I want to stay there and cuddle up. But I pull myself together just in time to see Kate HRH, and Zoe Knowall, from the corner of my eye. I despise her, I think. She sprays men's aftershave all over the place. She does everything wrong. She worries about us all the time.

Once a week, she brings us a bar of chocolate and puts it by our places on the table. Wednesday used to be *chocolate day*. 'Once a week is okay,' she'd say. The same goes for me, said dad. We used to like her shopping without us. She'd bring back little surprises, especially when we were sick — comics, beads, pens, stickers. Now, Tess sometimes sneers at the chocolate and leaves it on the table. Tess has an eighteen inch waist. Thomas, her ex, could put both hands round her waist and there'd be no gap. If it goes to eighteen and a half, or even eighteen and a quarter, she goes off on one. She goes back to bed for an hour and reads Stephen King. Then she gets up and jogs on the spot for two long minutes, swinging her arms about. She starts off all enthusiastic — all light and spry — then she starts to flag. Then she eats the chocolate. Then she gets a spot and she says, 'that fucking woman' and goes back to bed.

On the way back from Brent Cross, I'm trying to look out of the window and just drift, and she starts off again. Didn't I like Kate Swither then? Her mum had stopped to chat with her just the other day. Apparently the twins may have to stop eating kiwi fruit. It gives Lance hives, but if she gives some to Lot, he gets all jealous, and it's hard enough bringing up two kids with their father in the Gambia and all.

"Lancelot!" I laugh.

Moving on, she tells me about a tele programme she saw the other day about identical twins. They all said they were nothing like each other, didn't do the same things, and had different aspirations. Funny thing, she said, they used exactly the same words to deny their similarity. They had identical voices and were adamant in the same way. Then she starts in on John Lennon.

"You know, the Beatles?"

Gawd, the Beatles. It'll be Dean Martin in a minute. And she tells me it *again*. We'd seen it on the news.

This man was creating a right kerfuffle outside his house in Walthamstow. The police were there. He was shouting *this is not my 'ouse. I don't live 'ere! This ain't my wife. These are not my kids*. His poor wife, Joan, shrank into the background, but someone shoved a mike in her mouth. "*... e's been like this eversince that bloody trip to Noo York wiv the uver drivers. Says I'm not 'is missus... The police slammed 'im in the van and put him straight back on the plane 'ome. Tried to go back, didn't he? But 'e failed several of their visa requirements.*

"Mu-um," I say.

"*... and Joan says he'd never 'ad a guitar in his life... and didn't even like the Beatles.*

"He was a Gerry and the Pacemakers man." And she starts to sing. '*So ferry cross the water...*' right there on the 102, top deck. I throw her a filthy look.

"There was the Beatles, the Stones, and there was the Pacemakers. Now he's up all night prowling round the house, smoking weed, asking for herb teas, strumming, making notes. His voice has begun to sound uncannily like Lennons! He's even putting on a Liverpool accent, and he's never even *been* to Liverpool. Oh, and he wants a piano. A piano, if you don't mind. A white one!"

"Yes, Mum." I'm looking out of the window onto the busy London streets, thinking about Terry Lug. How his life must be worth something too — with his wife, and the little Lugs. And I'm thinking about mum, my mum. I've heard when people start to get old, they tell the same stories again and again. I look at mum. Is she starting to get old? A shudder goes down my back.

What mum doesn't realise is, I worry about her, just as much as she worries about me, specially now dad's gone. 'I'm glad he's gone,' she'd said. How I'd just stopped feeling so many things. It was like lopping off parts of my body. And walking around only half there. And everyone could see it, 'cept me...'

Mum goes out on her own all the time. She's only five foot three. *I'm* bigger than my mum. And *she* worries about me! I'm strong. I can run. I can jump down a whole flight of stairs. Mum gets tired after a quick shop at Tesco's. The other day, she rearranged her bedroom. Another fresh start. But in the middle of the night, she goes to the loo, and takes a running jump across the bedroom onto her bed, no longer there. We heard this enormous crash. 'God, Mum. ' Tess said. 'You're not fifty anymore!'

"You have to be alert," said mum, unpacking the bags. "That's the main thing."

And she runs upstairs and brings down a badge each, she'd had for zonx. *Be alert. The world needs all the lerts it can get.* We laugh. Group hug.

✿ ✿ ✿

"You two can have it," she says. "It's ugly. It's plastic. It controls the space and harmony... To watch it, I have to sit on the couch with my legs in front, and my neck twisted to the left for hours. It can't be good. You're not to watch it after the watershed."

"What's going on, mum?" asks Tess quietly, eyeing her ipad.

"We're a passive world of watchers. That's what we've become."

"Moi?" says Tess.

"Everyone, silly. We just sit back and let a spoiled few do the real living for us. They're just paraded before us. Off here, there, everywhere, wearing this ponsy dress and that. While we sit back — like we had no real selves. We're compelled to watch a few fortunate people having a great time — swanning off to the Oscars, premieres, tropical islands, making their crap fitness dvd's. While we slog away in our little lives. Just look at Charles the Second," (Beth from Bath's second husband, the first Charles having died in an unsolved pot-holing incident) "... putting his music out there on utube for years. Last time I looked, he had ten browsers. He's got grey hair now. Poor man." (Tess and I smile knowingly. Charlie's songs!!)

"Well," she goes on, "at least that period was better than his *"Elvis is still alive one!"* And she mutters, "utube has a lot to answer for. It's the modern equivalent of sandwich boards saying *the end is nigh.*

"We've become a society of useless watchers. Filled with junk food, junk movies, and drugs. Watching carcinogenic screens all day and all night. Totally passive! Our schools turn out glorified bank clerks and tour guides."

She then proceeds to tell us she's learning Chinese! She's always wanted to read Laozi in the original, so much being lost in translation. *And* she's going back to tap.

"You may not believe this girls, but I used to have good legs," she says thrusting a leg on Tess's desk.

"We don't believe it," says Tess.

✿ ✿ ✿

The doorbell goes. "Forgot about him," says mum. And in walks Jean-Louis Philippe Honore-Austere, or whatever. All open white shirt and teeth.

"He-lo," says Tess, under her breath, "where did you get him from?"

"Jean-Louis is from the language school up the road. He's going in the spare room, like he's waiting to be collected by Oxfam. "I have to give him three meals a week."

"Don't you mean a day?" I ask.

"No, she probably means a week," says Tess.

Mum takes Jean-Louis what's his face off to see his room.

"Okay," shouts Tess, squeezing her eyes, and punching me on the bruise she gave me yesterday. Mum comes back in alone.

"A hundred-and-thirty-five pounds a week" she mouths. "You two had better behave yourselves." Then the landline goes.

"Eet ees foer yo, Madame Vee-o-le," calls Jean-Louis Dun Fango, who has accustomed himself to the layout pretty damn quick, I'd say. Tess is so excited, we no longer have eye contact. Even I am thinking of what I will wear to our third meal of the day. *Vee-o-le* will have to buck her ideas up there, I can tell you. None of this cheese melted on toast lark, with an egg chucked on top, next to something that used to be vegetable and mineral, I can tell you. And if she thinks *I'm* making haute cuisine with camembert to follow, while she's off tapping, she can forget it.

✿ ✿ ✿

I hear mum on the phone. She's talking to Maggie. Who else?

'But you've tried it three times, Mags. Don't you think it's time to admit defeat?" Long pause. Maggie can talk for ten minutes without punctuation, a fag in one hand, while doing her nails, and never manage to ask mum how she is.

"Don't you realise," says mum, "most women *want* to be divorced. Marriage is just a *phase* we go through on our way to divorce. We inoculate ourselves with it, as protection against further outbreaks. It's our feminine seal of approval. Know what I mean...?

"I'll make time," she goes on. "Finish at four, four-thirty. Get home, see the girls, feed the Frenchman and out. I'm a free agent now. Thanks to Anus Erectus."

Another long pause.

"I don't know how you can say *that*," says mum, clearly irritated. Maggie usually manages to say at least three things every time she talks to mum, that mum is never going to forgive her for. "I worshipped the ground he *worked* on," laughs mum. "Must go now. We're settling in Sasha Distel." I can almost hear Maggie saying, 'Sasha who?' She's dead ignorant.

Polly East

Bucha

grief is a teardrop
sliding gently and deeply
into the crevice of your sadness
and our horror

I see the emblematic hand of freedom
rising upward from pools of blood
on city streets
of our European War

decades have passed
generations sipped their chilled wine
on honey-coloured beaches
enjoying   enjoying   enjoying

no hands dipped into
their peacetime treasure chest of pleasure
for now the price is butchered bodies
shattered homes and families

we have failed them
with the price still to be paid

grief lasts longer than peace

John Edwards

Painting the Accident

How to choose the palette
when all colours are absent
bar a ripple of cyan
on metal
when oblivion's magnet hauls her in

how to capture the rush
of the road
seeking her head?

Pick a brush. It must be broad
obsidian laden, will stride across
the canvas   no, thrash it,
with pitiless pigment
with grist of charred bones,
with the obliterating
history of impact

slap the black, twist the wrist,
stub the bristles as you lift,
let urgency speak
with turps and oil on the tongue

select the hue of shriek
for the thrown-over woman
pinioned by incidence

you'll need the sable
to string out her hair
across the blood-blotched road

how could the sun not
be purple, the son's face too,
fury-gorged at the rider
who thrust his mother —
her tender brains, his hearth of life's keys -
into an eruption of gods

squeeze the tubes for this - his

               yew   green falling
               bile   green rising

Stand. Away.   Reflect,
resist a glaze of wood ash grey
prefer to signal healing,
mix a wash of trumpet brass
to brush, blush the watching sky.

Angela Ellis

Snow Melt

We were a masterpiece of scratches / a patchwork of movement / blended until / I saw something that wasn't there / and always Brooklyn Bridge / peeking through / it's arches an echo of a collar / to choke me / if I thought about leaving

The blankness of waiting / pulled everything into my center / or towards the river / you'd asked me once / how well I could paint snow / the knife in your hand rippling / the hard butter / and the smell of burning bread / making me gag

Our marriage was a kind of whiteout / the promise of something just fallen / before it got messy / but you added blue and orange to the white / and everything turned grey / still I was frozen in place / always hoping for an early thaw

Walking alone / along the ice shelf / on an unformed morning / the ghosts / of the long shore men / sitting on their own hooks / with empty bellies and emptier eyes / asked me / whose side are you on / and I realized it was finally time / to be on my own

Adele Evershed

The Long Slow Road to Leaving

We are fastened to the sopping road by threads of rain — long and so slow — before seat-belts in back and quick belts for cheek — my Dad — a tip of a man — rubbed pink — shirt sleeves rolled passed his elbows — huffs and puffs about Sunday drivers — daft really because we all know it's Saturday — and Mam no longer held up by her apron strings drops her head on the window — to stare at Fern Hill gently ebbing in farewell — saying — husht let's just enjoy the view now — and me and my brother scrapping and scribbling through our I-Spy books — measure the road in miles of sheep and milk cow roundabouts — and then look — a red kite flyover — look there see — pulling over in a lay-by for dinner at twelve o'clock sharp — fish paste sandwiches and orange pop — more thrilling than old Pen-y-Fan — Dad shaking off the storm of him and giving Mam a cwtch — saying — look now see — the land of your fathers — and it's Mam's turn to huff as he starts to sing — rumbling like snow off a roof in a child's wish for Christmas — and we get back in the car itching to be there — and we twist and we turn and my brother feels sick — I think maybe I spot a red deer and mark it in my book without telling him — and we ask — when will we get there?

and get told — we'll be there in a minute now — after the longest minute we arrive with the strawberry moon — red and green and right as rain — but the key breaks in the boot so we can't brush our teeth — and I sleep in my knickers — yet it's the best holiday ever — and then Dad leaves...

Adele Evershed

Chiaroscuro

My mother has been painting the Sinai desert
in Saint Luke's Sunday school classrooms. She writes,
Did one camel I like and another I'm not happy with.
A wall of sheep in Zion Lutheran got her picture
in the paper, but when the new pastor moved himself
to tears with his sermons, she switched to Saint Luke's.
Home for Christmas, I flip through photos of her murals
in the classrooms of my old elementary school:
blue earth suspended in formless space, Pangea
spread across its face; blond Adam with a mullet
and a shorter, darker Eve. Her best is of Noah's Ark,
with pairs of storybook giraffes, leopards and elephants.
Christmas morning she doesn't go to church and I don't ask.
We take the dogs for a walk instead. Unleashed, her two
poodles disappear in three feet of snow. *I bought white ones,*
she says, *because I thought they'd be easy to see in the dark.*

Lara Frankena

Corona Daze

according to the latest text, Patsy-Ann is coming
in Raspberry Van and there are no missing items
translation: I can drink tonight!

          as I have been   every night
          since lockdown homeschool began

daytimes I send the children into trees with books
so they'll have something to do away from me

          the health survey asks if I drink,
          and *If so, how frequently?*

of course, they often need help getting up
getting down, retrieving a fallen book

          I select *occasionally*, type
          a few glasses of wine per week

or they need me to pass them a water bottle

          by which I mean nightly
          usually after my husband goes to bed

but at ground level I might achieve
a few minutes' peace on a picnic blanket

          he doesn't drink, which makes me look bad
          next question: *Do you ever drink alone?*

for some reason
their shoes tend to fall out of trees

          I am tempted to answer *always*
          but strictly speaking, that's not true

narrowly missing me

Evonne rolled a beer to me
as we sat six feet apart in her back garden

even though I brought them
rocket-shaped real fruit & veg lollies
in a cooler bag stuffed with every ice pack we own

which I entered via a side gate
propped open in anticipation of my arrival

chunks of melting sludge
slip from lolly sticks

a generous 500 ml cylinder of beer
which rolled rather well

adding claret and chartreuse stains
to the stripy blanket

a little too generous for my bladder
so I had to exit via that side gate within the hour

that I have every intention of washing
when these kids go back to school

and run all the way home

Lara Frankena

Icons

Long abstracts of the human face,
blackened and old.
Ovals and curves express a grace,
remote and cold,

as if a candle lights the dark
in high relief,
incising faces with a stark,
sinuous grief.

Gold discs and crescents, burnished spoons
of holiness,
the halos round their heads are moons
that almost kiss.

Madonna holds her seated Christ
upon her arm.
Out on the limb of her tense wrist,
he is her psalm.

Her face tilts down to greet his lips
but she stares past
us, looking to the dark eclipse
and the lots cast.

Icons are flowers from a far
country's rich dirt
somewhere inside of us. They are
rooted in hurt,

the bitter soils of it crumbling
on lips – a share
of black bread for silent mumbling
like a prayer.

Jim Friedman

Here on Earth / Out There in Space

Baby Heidi, two weeks early,
blooms unimaginably precious,
jostles worlds aside to make way.

Born jaundiced, she doesn't open
her bowels for forty-eight hours
post-partum, and her latching-on

is slightly off target — she growls
and grizzles a lot — we express
concern, but the nurse reassures:

*Crying's good, I'd rather hear her
protesting than being too quiet.*
But they keep her in — so time drags

in a broken, heart-in-mouth night,
as Heidi basks in therapeutic, blue light.

In the evening of Saturn's day, Heidi inherits the earth, comes trailing
luminous hopes with night coming on, with those endeared fraught with
love until she fills her nappy, and all the while all the universe wheels
absolutely like those rings of Saturn bound to their moon-breaker,
debris of an overly intimate moon, ice-brilliant as if celebrating breakage
— and, in the whole of creation, spacetime glows…

and, as the antibiotics
strengthen, her eyes are opener,
gazier than three days ago,

frankly quizzical: look, how she
looks and looks! Accepting, being
accepted, while galaxies turn.

And the deep field image of the bright-eyed empyrean, barely delivered from its void, is rife with relics of fourteen billion years ago, glutted with original energies, Time realising that it is being lit by the purest fire, the desert awaking to discover it has turned into an unprecedented garden, a cosmos collateral with the wonder which its newest creature will grow to feel.

I think I can remember a Christmas morning:
I was six or seven, innocent of the time,
no idea — but it's dark I think, still dark,
yet the sort of dark where dawn has its foot in the door.
Has he been? Has he? Hoping the weight
on my bed is a yes, I still can't open my eyes
as one glimpse could forestall or abort the spell,
and something would die. So, eyes nine-tenths closed,
I'm deeply enthralled, not really for the sake of presents,
but more because this means magic happens,
and the world is matter-of-fact with miracle
encompassing me, having my heart at its heart.

One learns otherwise, of course: things
are not charmed — though there may be times,
a hoard-able horde of moments,

that briefly derail the mundane:
supernovae, or suns new-born,
or the rings of Saturn, round as an iris,

as an iris — just like grandchildren growing
feels like moons in ever-loosening orbits.

Lindsay Fursland

the waiting room

her daughter has winnowed
her treasures down to
four small paintings
and two items of furniture —
the antique globe wine bar
and the davenport

both stand empty of the memories
she had stored for a lifetime

an institutional dresser
detains her smalls
restrains petticoats
and stockades compression socks
for ankles which seep
with melancholy

she has gin
she thinks
in a drawer somewhere
but she forgets
to drink it
in the lavender fog
of the waiting room

as she waits
she prays

but God
she says

is not listening

Siobhan Gifford

The Hit-count

She's put Trixie in the drawer \ alongside blurred memories \ and some neatly-folded remnants \ of the person she used to be \ into which she can no longer fit. \ When did she last try them on, \ a final dance before the mirror of imaginary men?

It doesn't matter, \ the Internet is her scrapbook.

In the supermarket chiller aisle \ she watches mothers wanting more hands \ to control trollies and children \ as both slip through their clumsy fingers \ finesse and subtlety long since abandoned. \ Scanning for grated Cheddar \ she wonders if they're really looking \ for escape, or salvation, or love. \ And as they walk away \ slack-bottomed in too-loose jeans \ she categorises shapes as if a pastime: \ 'child-bearing hips' \ (the hips she had; the children she didn't). \ Lifting Mozzarella by mistake \ dropping it carelessly into a basket \ whose contents now define her, \

she remembers what they used to say.

Her breasts were all adjectives.

But now they too succumb. \ Too far gone for a comeback. \ With a pang \ she imagines Newton and Old Father Time \ sniggering in the corner of the room \ all the while she was humping, \ moaning, licking lips at lenses, \ going through the motions.

More tit, Love. More tit!

She avoids cameras now \ much as she avoids that bottom drawer, \ yet weakens just occasionally to check the hit-count \ on the film of which she is most proud —\ and where she imagines 'film' spoken with reverence \ as if she were Streep or Taylor or Oscar-bound.

Nearly two million. \ At least that's one thing \ that won't be destroyed by time.

Ian Gouge

How are you?

How are you? Fine, I say,
which is rubbish
it's been the most terrible day.

Lovely weather isn't it, the roses,
hydrangeas, how gorgeous they look!
Yes, it's a lovely summer, I say
   (thinking)
     But roses are triffids, hydrangeas corpse flowers,
     They smother the earth, they block my way.

How was the op?
Went well, I murmur
   (thinking)
     But it's left my brain a soft, sticky mush,
     And the world a bewildering, morphing blur.

How are the boys?
Doing well, I say
   (thinking)
     They're dads now, they've got their own lives
     In unreachable cities, far away.

So where are you going?
I don't know, I say,

Who are you going with?
I don't know, I say,

What'll you do?
I don't know, I say

I know nothing,

But grief, dressed up as pain,

And I'm not fine.

Diana Hills

I am ninety-eight

I am ninety-eight.
"You look so well" they say — *but*

my knotted, twisted hands can't grip
those packs and potions, hiding in their plastic prison.
My swollen, sore and battered feet can't shuffle
to the far, far distance of that non-slip mat.

I am ninety-eight.
"What a treasure" they say — *but*

my back's bent like a broken hula hoop
long abandoned in a neglected garden.
Unbidden from my hissing ears come sounds
like whooshing waves on Brighton beach.

I am ninety-eight.
"Hello, my lovely" they say — *but*

my mind's a swirling, whirring wheel of memory,
Friends forgotten, foes remembered, loves adored.
I cry for past time lost on worthless work,
why slave to that avenging god, fake wealth?

I am ninety-eight,
"You're no trouble" they say.— *but*

I leak, I soil, my pull-on jumper's stained
where once lush breasts spilled from velvet dresses.
No socks or shoes adorn my feet
once shorn in black stockings, sky high stilettos.

I am ninety-eight.
"Be safe and keep inside" they say — *but*

captive now in four grey walls
the world outside seems lost forever.
Stars and moon that once heard laughter, chatter,
still shine, though barely glimpsed through half-blind eyes.

I am ninety-eight,
"Keep going" they say — *but*

she who once was daughter, mother, lover,
freedom fighter turned to keyboard tapper,
lingers now in that sepulchral place
the crowded, waiting room for death.

I am ninety-eight,
let me escape forever, I cry out loud,
leave me still and do not wake me,
my time is done, I've no place here.
Whatever lies beyond, I do not fear,
old age is not for wimps or weaklings, and I am they.

Diana Hills

He has always been in your house. He crawled into your life and sits in your brain like the tumour he resembles. This... mass. He eats your food, sleeps in your bed, wetly cooing to you with his many mouths. "Come on, pet. I'm hungry..." You know he doesn't just want food. He wants a chase, he wants you to be afraid.

Red like old blood, bulging and pulsating with intent, it pulls itself through the kitchen towards you. He had wandered in from his — *your* — room, pushing your bowl aside and drags you to your feet. He likes the kitchen as a starting point. He let the kitchen go to waste. Pale counters and wooden walls dusty and damp, the glass hob crusted with sauces and discoloured crumbs. They don't look edible now, and if you try to clean them he'll say you're messing with things. So you leave it. You let it go to ruin, a pigsty fit for someone as worthless as you and a monster like... him.

The chase is always from there. Sometimes after breakfast, sometimes when you get yourself a drink. He doesn't do it all the time. He wants to surprise you, wants to keep the game fresh. You run. He slithers. He says the same thing as always: "I'm coming to get you, pet."

Thundering blood fills your ears. You're *sick* of this, but the danger is still there. He will *hurt* you, so you run. In this moment you are reduced to instinct, avoiding pain. "Leave me alone..." You mutter back. "Tired..."

"Ha... you love the game, don't be coy. You're always tired!"

"Nh... no. Still hungry." Your throat is dry.

"Oh, shut up! You'll eat when I've eaten — now..." He breathes in through his mouths, calming down, or trying to. He wants to enjoy himself. He wants to lie to itself and believe that you're enjoying this too. "Now, start *running*."

Maybe he'll be kind for once, you think. Or you would have the first time. You know him... it, well enough. The scars on your body prove it. Your belly, your arms, your face. He doesn't need to hide what he does to you. He thinks you're all his.

You run, scrambling away. He crawls on the stolen hands of the people he already played its game with. Bones poking through digested digits on a carpet filthy with his slime and other clutter. You wonder if his voice is just whatever is left of his playmates. Vocal chords and lungs not quite eaten yet. They still have some use.

You rush past the living room, the carpet squelching on your bare feet — he took your shoes along with most of your clothes. Just threw them out because 'well, you don't need them, silly'. He lets you get to the door, lets you fiddle with the doorknob and the many locks. Your hands shake, rattling the chain. You hear him gurgle and laugh.

A bony hand touches the small of your back. He presses his finger in. It's a dull pain, followed by a sharp one as a layer of skin is eaten away. The spot feels raw as he smothers you. He doesn't touch you more than that, but he fills your air with his presence. "Too slow, pet." You feel his breath on your neck. He moves your hair out of the way so that you feel he — hair's gotten long. He says you need it cut, but he won't let you out.

You hear the small, wet noise of his lips parting, all his mouths grinning. "Can't have you wandering off, now can I? Don't want you walking out on me again."

"Didn't... won't leave you..." You don't want him to be mad. You placate the beast.

"Of course you won't, pet."

He drags you further into the house, away from your freedom. *Your* freedom. You... there's no one in your world but him and you. The freedom might as well belong to you. He wouldn't use it, certainly. He *has* it. He can leave. He... you hate him. He is all you have and you hate him with everything else in your heart. The bits of you he hasn't twisted and infected and tried to mould into his 'pet'.

You'd hoped this day would be one of those where he simply left you alone. You would be left to your books, keeping out of its way. And then he started talking to you. This is your world, your days, your weeks, your months. You can't remember what the outside of your own house looks like, but at least you... no. It's not good enough. Just saying 'no' doesn't stop him.

Do. Something. You're tired of... all of this.

...

"Morning Rob." You hear a voice outside. The monster is coming home from... wherever he goes. The door locks behind him. Your world is still small but at least he's not there to fill it. 'Rob' is what the voices outside call him. He doesn't use names with you. He just calls you... 'pet', or 'silly', or 'you little piece of —' no. He wouldn't let you repeat something like that.

"Morning." You press your ear to the door, seeing a sliver of light beyond. The hallway is dark and clogged with your own smell.

"How you doing?"

You can make out him grumbling. "Can't complain. The dog's giving me trouble. You know how they get."

"Ah, yeah." The voice sounds knowing. And... dog? You don't feel like a dog. "Maybe let him out of the house some time? Never see him."

"She's shy. Don't blame her."

"Ah," a pause. "Right. Well, what you been up to?" You struggle to remember the stranger's face. It's been a long time since you left the house. You would talk to him about the weather. He had a child. You would wish him well, perhaps try to get friendly with him, see if he wanted to come to the pub some time.

You would like that idea very much. A simple walk to the pub. A pint of beer. You would give anything for that. He won't let you drink. He hordes the 'good stuff' like a dragon hoarding gold. A monster sitting in his own filth and possessions.

That's just an idea. Make it happen... soon. You've an idea, but it can't be now. *Make it happen!* You scurry back to the living room, the curtains drawn. The floor is still sticky. You know where the knives are! Go, get them, hide one?

No, it wouldn't work. He would find it — your back hurts from before. You scratch at it, skin flaking off. The chase wasn't long ago. He'll want to go again. He... he ruins you. Tears you up and leaves you to crawl on. This fear twists into hatred. You feel your body burn from the inside. You feel tense, like you're discovering a secret. You're thinking up something horrible and wonderful.

Hungry, you think, *make him food.*

As if on cue, he is here, in your home again. Your respite is ended. Already he is pushing himself into you, patting your shoulder. "Nosy little man. Can't keep me away from you forever." He chuckles.

You feel choked by his redness, but you manage to force the words out in a cheerful tone. "I know, dear. Um... I'd... I can cook you something to eat. You're... I want to make you happy."

You use simple words in a soft, gentle tone. You want it to sound convincing. If it doesn't work he'll be mad. He'll see through it. Your heartbeat picks up again. You don't want any more pain. He pushes past you, your shoulder burning at his touch. The pain makes you wince, but he doesn't pay he any heed. "What's the occasion, pet?"

"Nothing just... I know you're mad at me. I want to make it up to you." You smile at the back of his... head isn't the right word. It's hard to tell his real shape. You think you can see the skull of one of his previous playmates bobbing around in his soupy mass. The black sockets look back at you. You're looking at your own fate.

"No, that can't be it. You... what are you hiding?" The skull's mouth opens, he tilts on its side. The contents of his body are churning as he thinks.

"Nothing!" You don't shout, shouting makes it worse. "I just... I just... I don't —"

"Okay, okay — okay — okay! I *get* it. Just... one word's enough." He pulls his bulk into the kitchen. "What were you making?" You can't see his eyes, if he has any, but he turns as if he's looking around.

You walk in behind him, his stink and slime making you want to wretch. You want to be rid of him... but you stifle your disgust. You've been doing that for a long time, what's one more night? The process is long: You slave over the stove, preparing something simple. You know how to cook. You remember your mother teaching you. Years ago now. Use it. Use this memory, something better than this. Ignore the pain, ignore his leering, his grumbles. The knife is in the wooden rack. A big one. A steak knife. It's clean, sharp. You imagine him splitting open. Him screaming, begging, wailing like the baby he is — yes! That, more of that! End it! End he —

"Ey, what's taking you so long?" He's looking at you. You were lost in thought. He sounds impatient. "Y' said food and now I'm starving. Look what y' did to me!" He laughs.

You laugh back. It's safe to laugh if he's doing he too. The steam heats up your face. You're sweating, but not just from that. You feel tense. Always so tense. When he's gone you can breathe properly — focus on that. And the food. Don't drop it. He'll hate that you were so clumsy. He'll push your face in the spillage and make you eat it.

The meal is simple. Pasta and sauce. Some cheese on the side. You feel your arm hair stand on end at the sound of his slurping and munching. His mouths make a chorus of noises, all worming their way into your ears. You want to cover them, but you need to focus. You're behind him. He's not looking at you — do it! Do it now — now — now!

The knife doesn't slide in. It's jammed into his... you hesitate to call it a neck. You hear yourself wail as you rip the blade out, driving it back in, deep. This... you *have* to do this. Fingers numb, blood rushing in your veins, you *stab* him.

He flounders in his chair, a flailing mess of slime and gurgling mouths. You think he's trying to curse at you, but he doesn't come out right. He spits blood in your face, grabbing your head and shoving you away. Even dying, he's stronger. Even when you take back your strength, he is stronger.

You feel your body collide with the doorway. Wooziness hits you like a bucket of cold water. Squinting, you push yourself forward — end him now, or him simply won't end! You'll be stuck with this monster! The acid eats at you as you rush forward, plunging the knife and your arm further inside him. You tear into his core, his mouths letting out a scream that bounds off the tiles of the kitchen.

He stains the flood, his body eating into he floor — it's over so quickly. You ignore the stains. You ignore the pain in your arm, your chest. You leave the mess that used to be him, walking towards the door. You can't ignore the pain now, but you move in spite of it. You have the time to unlock the door. The world is blindingly bright. You shield your eyes.

You feel elated. Free

Ben Hramiak

A Priest's Thoughts

The truly good ones soon
Burn out, consumed by a
Quick flame.
I think about them often
Through the sirens and screams
Of the late-night crowd
Beyond the rectory walls.
It wasn't that they didn't
Find the meaning that
They sought,
But too much of it
Coursed through them,
Carving the notches
Of experience to their
Weak frames.

It is easy to help a man
When you can see his wounds.
Any fool with eyes can
Make it his job to tend them,
But what of when it is
Internal, their pain?
How do we minister those
With no sense of self,
Who see only mere matter
In their mirror each day.
That will break down
Quickly if they're lucky,
More likely now, the
Decay will take time,
Unless there is an illness,

To them, what do you say?

Tom Larner

For O

His spleen, engorged with blood,
Had burst, freeing the cancerous
Cells, which, sped by the
Explosion, attached themselves
To organs, found plinths
On the rough bone, and beds
In the arteries, the tides
Of blood which surged there
Called them home.

The clots of hair and sweat
Pulsed his quick, shallow
Breaths on the few times
That he walked. Mostly he lay,
Indifferent to our strokes.
We saw the hollow cage
For his heart
Where they had shaved him.

We had time to notice,
Listening only to the wind's
Unrest outside our thin walls
And knowing that
For him its song would never end.

                                        Tom Larner

Pier in the Rain

All frenzy done. Cinema curtain waves are silken on sand,
closing down, the sea steel grey, the clouds gritty charcoal,
halo mist hovers over distant water, hills loom like mountains,

rain shrouds the coast. With her white brolly tussling with gusts
the Japanese print of her is minimalist, monochrome,
offshore wind at her back, the North Sea suppliant,

every step on the pier is defiant of sense, a joy to the senses,
frame of chiaroscuro with a hint of sepia, all colour drained.
Rain rivets the pier. On close inspection divots are crowns

like pennies thrown from the sky, the pier a running stream.
The colour of January, the colour of Whitby, is a brooch
she pins in her mind, on her old coat, the day after epiphany.

S.J. Litherland

Abu Kammash, Libya

From the shallows, beryl-blue shades to deepwater cobalt.
Dazzling white stones and water reflections make it impossible to look
unless you raise your eyes far out to sea.
Nets stretched, drying, are repaired by unspeaking men
sitting with their backs to the sun.
Roped pots line up, designed to make an octopus feel quite at home
until yanked to the surface.

On the hills loom Turkish forts offering granite shade,
silent watchers over a parched panorama.
As the swell sweeps in and out, a graveyard of wrecked boats
clunk, clatter and scrape.
In the distance, ageing vessels chug by, low in the water with many passengers
and these days the fishermen are adjusting to separating the bodies of children
from the rest of their catch.

Ann Logan

Be Nice

You say *I love you*
like it's an apology.

You give me your door key:
a symbol of commitment.

You let me slap you around the face
as if it's supposed to make me feel better.

You worry when I don't answer,
then give me nothing but white noise.

You just can't make up your mind
like you can't make up wrongdoing with love

when it is only a word.

Carmina Masoliver

Awesome

Somehow
when I step in this door
Something
is left behind.
Life's litter blows away across the grass.

Somewhere
in a momentary eclipse
an aqua realm of water opens
lifting me, to and fro, in the surge of
words that paint
paint that rhymes
stitches that cross and knot.
I am adrift on a swirling eddy
of infinite possibilities
that reach to take my hand
or elude a finger touch
as they slide into horizon blue.

Somewhat
enraptured, I deep dive
into this entrancing water world
where pen and brush
snorkel their way down
to rocks that give up their sound
and fronded weeds their hidden lives
words shell: paint shingles
stitches unpick their patterning.
Until, needing to breathe,
I call the dive,
ascending, feet flicking, above.

Someplace
where the garden fork leans against a garage wall
where spiders spin on dusty boxes
and there's a very cold cup of tea
that's been waiting for
Sometime

Caroline Matusiak

A Message

'I'm getting flowers. Lots of flowers. I'm thinking keen gardener. Pardon? Speak up a bit, please. Ah — Rose. Not just the flower. No? Right. Okay. I understand. Is there a Rose here anywhere?'

No one put up a hand. It always felt awkward when this happened. I half wanted to pretend my name was Rose. I did believe in it, well, I wanted to, but surely they could get it wrong sometimes, have an off night. This was the third time I'd been and hadn't been called on. It left me lower than when I came. Still, you can't expect it, they say. You have to be patient. And open.

'My mam's name's Rose. She couldn't come tonight. She wanted to, though.'

A thin woman with straight blonde hair had spoken. People turned to look, briefly.

'That's smashing, my love. Well, I'm getting a message for Rose. Does your mam have anyone who's passed over into spirit? He says he's not been here long.' The medium turned to the side and spoke to someone invisible nearby on the stage. 'Alfred, is it? Or Fred?' She turned back to the audience, to the lady who'd spoken. 'Has your mam lost an Alfred, my love?'

'That was our dog, that was.'

A few people tittered. Some older members stared at the offenders, stony faced. These were newbies, obviously. Just in out of curiosity before the pub.

'Ah, you see, sometimes they talk about pets, isn't it. Well, look now. It's the dog, is it? Right you are. Spaniel — I've got him by here. You're a tidy thing, aren't you?'

'Yes, our Alfred. You've got him. Lovely dog he was, aye. Gentle as a baby.'

'Right, love. I'm getting a bit more now. Just a moment. What's that you say? Frank? Francis?'

The blonde lady shook her head. Her eyes brimmed with sorrow. Her face puckered. I thought she might start crying at any moment. It had happened the first time I'd come, and they'd taken the person out the back — given them an early tea and a slice of cake, apparently.

61

The meeting was growing restless, chairs scraping, throats clearing. It was nearly time for the break, when they'd wheel an urn in and the home-made cakes would be divvied up.

'Get on with it,' the man next to me said, under his breath. He smelt of stale booze. I always had bad luck sitting next to people. His leg ran alongside mine. A big bloke. No sense of personal space. We were cramped in.

'He's fading, love. I can't quite. Do you want to go now? Is it? Aye, my love. Don't you worry now. Alfred the dog is alright, and so are you. That's good, my darlin.' Then, to the audience: 'They do that sometimes. Little bit shy. I'm thinking it wasn't too long ago, you see, love. Am I right?'

I looked across and the blonde lady's head was bowed. She nodded, and a single sob burst from her. A woman in the next seat put an arm around. 'It's alright, babe,' she said.

The room was semi-dark. They had dimmers on the lights. And at the back of the little stage it was almost black. I must have imagined it, but for a moment I thought I could see a faint outline of a smallish dog. It moved across the back and into the deep red side curtains. Just a shadow, obviously. And the atmosphere. You pick up on it. I wouldn't have said anything.

I chatted with a few people over my tea and fruitcake. Coming to these meetings was a way of getting out since it happened. Bryn never would have approved before. And I probably never would have gone; no reason, except for our Dad, and decades had passed there. You got all kinds here. Some surprisingly young — tattoos, piercings, the lot. Taking it all very seriously. As I wanted to. As I needed to. If only I'd be called. Just a word would do. Just a word of forgiveness. It would mean everything to me.

We all settled back in our chairs, and Alice, the lady that organises the mediums and takes money at the door, gave out the notices, including about the annual party.

Gladys, the evening's guest medium, came back on stage as the lights lowered. *Just let me know you forgive me*, I thought. *That's all I ask. Just a soothing word, and I'll try and move on.* I tried to make myself as emotionally open as possible. To accept anything that came.

Sally, who I knew from my job at Asda, had a nice message from her gran, telling her that moving house was a good idea, and not to worry about breaking that vase, that she'd never liked it anyway. Gladys then went into her concentrating mode, as I thought of it. I watched her face, which seemed to change in the low light. Other features passed across it, is all I'll say. Then she opened her eyes wide and said in a deeper and stronger voice than before: 'You're next!' She was looking bothered by what she'd said, and tried to cover it with a laugh.

'Sorry, my loves. That can happen, when the spirit is particularly troubled. They can come through you like a dose of salts. And there's nothing you can do about it. He's still here, though. He's nearby. Who do you want to speak to, my lovely? Oh, he's angry — he's fair tamping. What's wrong there? Is there a message you want to give?'

I began to feel very uneasy. A chill went right through me. I thought about leaving — just getting up and barging past the knees, and out into the fresh air, never to return. The voice Gladys had used, it reminded me of him. Not exactly, but it had that hardness he sometimes used when he lost his rag. Which wasn't that often, to be fair.

'I'm a getting a B,' said Gladys. She scanned the audience, looking for a bite. 'No, it's coming now. It's a Bryn — for definite. A Bryn wants to speak to someone here.'

My mouth went dry. I raised my hand. 'I've lost a Bryn,' I said. 'It was an accident. He just went off...very annoyed with me one night. And the car came off the road. Up near Crumlin it was.'

'Right, my love, I see,' said Gladys. 'Well, he's a bit annoyed still, I'm sorry to say. Aren't you, love? What do you want to say now? Is there any message, some crumb of comfort you can bring?'

'I'm so sorry, Bryn.' It exploded out of me. It was like we were alone in the place, just Gladys and me and the spirit of my dead husband. No one else mattered. This might be the last chance I'd get. 'I didn't love him, Bryn. Not like you. It was just a silly stupid thing. A one-off. I didn't care about him at all. I just felt lonely with you working all the time, and the pub at weekends...we hardly ever...' I could hear intakes of breath around me, and mutterings, but I didn't care.

Back home, I opened a bottle of wine. It was one of Bryn's. His favourite from Asda. Well, it was Argentinian, actually. Lately, I've taken to having a few glasses before bed, to stave off the dreams, you know.

Bryn had gone quiet on Gladys after my outburst. Couldn't blame him really. I could imagine his face: *you're showin me up again.* He could be awful pompous when he had a mind. But I did love him, see. That's no lie. And he knows it. Wherever he is.

In bed, I drew the covers up to my face. Life alone isn't all it's cracked up to be. Freedom can feel like a terrible weight. Don't wish for something, they say. You might just get it.

You're next. Must've been him saying that. For me. I'm next. Well, I didn't drive, so it couldn't mean that. And of course I would go eventually, but not for a while yet, surely. Whenever I thought about meeting someone else, I felt empty inside. Like I didn't have the right, see. No. All that was over with. I'd had my chances.

As I was slipping away into my sleep, I saw this big red heart. It was like a painting but it was also alive. Throbbing with energy — love, perhaps — or just blood.

My sister found me two days later. She had a spare key, and I hadn't answered her texts or phone calls. I watched her face. She didn't cry. But I could tell she was shocked. We'd never been that close.

I watched her pick up the photograph of Bryn and me off the cabinet. She stood looking at it, with a twist to her mouth. 'You took her in the end, you bastard,' she said.

Mark Mayes

self is other

lately, you move through days
like some mud creature through mud,
yet mud is not your element;

do you even have an element?
when people claim water, air, fire, earth
with such instant certainty,
both for self and others;
self is other;

R D Laing is on your lips,
though what he said now lost to books
you drunk when you were young enough
to be called young
by self and others;
self is other;

lately, you glom on to the nearest convenience,
whether open, operable, stocked, or humanly clean;
the urge may grip at any time,
the routine to solve it
now like any other old routine,
once belonging to self, and still to others;
self and others; self is other

Mark Mayes

the material world

fading flower pattern
empty now
and folded, enfolded

you lost your luggage
word by word

the buttons that close you
some fell away on threads
or no thread

I fill you now
at night
as once I filled you

the old tissue
stained and clumping

you cover lost me
as the nights chill
as the end stalks near

you lost your second language
returned to sound
and dear heartbreaking repetition
some precious bird

I pull you over my face
behind misted windows
breathe in what specks of you
exist still here

you laundered you
pressed flowers under hot irons
the heat you gave
pulsing down the years

Mark Mayes

Event

Looking up
she found the window frame
a-swarm with snowflakes

as if the whole family
had arrived by chance together
for some reunion.

Penny McCarthy

No dancing in Ireland

From father to son, and son again, the fiddle was passed along,
And all the jigs and hornpipes, and all the slow sad songs

Have polished it with playing, and worn out many a string,
And many a hand is dust now that once had made it sing.

Of the fiddlers in Casey's family, some played sweet and some played strong,
But none compared with Casey, who I loved his whole life long.

He fiddled for his supper at the big house on the hill,
And the gentlemen and ladies, they praised him for his skill.

He fiddled his way into the heart of every hopeful girl,
He fiddled at his own wedding — you should've seen the dancers twirl.

But no child came to bless them and carry the music on,
In spite of all the candles they lit to get a son.

So now the fiddle hangs silent on Casey's widow's wall,
And for me there's no dancing left in Ireland at all.

Emmaline O'Dowd

Sedimentary

every weaponized word
festers beneath
the earth's surface
and cements itself
into a single
sedimentary stone
seething with
self-loathing,
and the slightest
inconvenience
sends the stone
spiraling towards
my self-esteem,
a glass house
painted to appear
like brick —

on impact,
i am elemental
once more.
i am sand
slipping through fingers
too small
to scoop it
back together.

i am nothing.

Alfie Ormsbee

A Boy and His Dog

Paused, motor idling, I gaze through my windshield at a standing dog. This story is not about that elegant creature. Not about its dark, trim, muscular body, long legs, and black pointy nose bred for the chase & smell of the chase — not the same kind of horrific hunt I read of today on-line.

The canine stands, pointed ears perked up, alert to a young man with brownish-blond hair, freckled fair skin and muscular legs under his loose & shiny shorts — taking a break as the June-warm cools down, leaving remote work — abandoning his laptop — to gift his dear dog with going out.

Hours earlier I read of a boy — near age for high school graduation — taking three weapons — AR 15 included (keep reading — the story gets better) strolling on a sidewalk, then stepping onto grass among the three-bedroom houses with pastel paint jobs kept up well. So many well-polished SUVs, sedans or pickups parked in front.

The boy hunted indiscriminately. He blasted whatever adult or school child chanced near his course. Perhaps a woman bends to settle a briefcase in her shiny Prius? Or a man grips a hose to spray thirsty roses with an extra sip of water. Or two girls gossiping as they stroll to class. Did envy for a sunshiny smile catalyze his lonely, consuming rage?

An officer opened his door — even the dark-uniform-sleeved hearts were within the mad-boy's aim to bloody. Soon the gun-savvy high schooler the bullet he craved pierced his scrawny chest. His strange reasons remain secret, still swarm in his grave.

My red-light moments pass swiftly as I stare. My young man stoops to lightly, streak fond fingers down sleek, chocolate fur. The furious boy floats in and out of my inner gaze.

Pivoting focus, I imagine what the strawberry youth whispers in his best friend's soft ear. What sweets words grace his speech? Maybe, *that a boy. Good dog. You're great!* I watch him enfold his dog with fond arms. Lightness softens my chest. He scratches behind the pooch's soft and floppy ears.

All at once, boys and young men seem not so fearsome. Or full of hate. Their needs not so mysterious. Maybe most males crave some creature giving or welcoming touch. Need to be god-like to a pair of eyes.

The signal flashes green. The pet leaps from the curb — an inward whistle as at a starting block has freed him. His beloved hustles gladly after, his baggy, red nylon shorts a flapping. Two parallel, straight lines — unbroken and unsullied — border them.

Carol Park

Hours to Keep

In the days
When we got the Summer stoned
And love was yet to show
Its ropes and pulleys
We roared like Northern looms
Each tomorrow
Was a page ripped out
Our yesterdays
A tooth under the pillow

Now
Clock hands sweep like radar lines
Faint pulses
On the margins of a life
Caught in the amber
And when silence wakes us early
It dawns
Every nest becomes
Just a flown from thing
When the growing up
Is done

Jonty Pennington-Twist

Pas De Deux
(for my mother)

We must let each other keep
The pieces of ourselves
We gave
To stop the other bleeding out

And we must give each other back
The quiet truths
That our unspokens
Spoke so rudely over

And you must give me back
The years
I was someone else's boy

And I must give you back
The surplus heartbeats
Of your youth

And in time
I must take with me
As much of you as I can carry
And I must hold it
In a broken heart
As gently as I would
A baby bird

Jonty Pennington-Twist

Gerunds

Parts of speech are active
making
meaning
in gaps between words

Silence is perceptible only
if you know what is
being

said: Your looking
is not the same as my seeing
or Christ knows
as his knowing

The world is not impressed

a passive voice, mine may be thought of

My writing on water, on sand,
on leaves
in a book's binding
is whispering to hearing, needing, aiding

my living
is persisting
exploring
geology of folding
cortex smoothed by passing

time and ineffably
being

no one can mine the treasure

Mine

My loving, striving, reordering,
reshaping, recording

Remembering.

                                              Susan Perkins

"The work of writing [is] very close to the job of being: by creative reflection
and awareness to help life itself live in me" — *Entering the Silence: Becoming a
Monk and Writer*, Thomas Merton, 1996

"The English gerund is identical in form, but only in form, with the active
present participle." — *The New Fowler's Modern English Usage*, 3rd ed (Burchfield)

It's not always easy to know where to start a story. It is not necessarily when it begins. Perhaps this one begins in a dame school in Monkton-on-Sea, where a motherless boy read more than was meant in the smiles of a girl who might have been his sister if all were known. But I shall start it in our own time. That is where we live.

A couple — Julian and Alex — are toasting the New Year, looking forward to the day at the end of March when they will open the doors to the Star of the Sea. It will be Monkton's first restaurant with rooms, and they are well on the way to completing the restoration of the derelict tavern near the seafront, not far from the marina. They have hired a chef, have negotiated deals with local fishermen and butchers, and they are confident that 2020 will be their year. They are tipsy with excitement and exhilaration at what they have achieved.

'Tell you what,' says Alex, 'you remember when people said this place should be pulled down? That no one can make a go of it? That that's why we got it so cheap? I reckon the final thing we need to put into the mix is local history, local mystery, stuff. I've been looking things up — in real life, not just online — and the Star of the Sea goes all the way back to the time of the monks. There was a church nearby dedicated to the Virgin Mary. But In Cromwell's time that church was defiled, and the troops stayed here, and ever since it's been cursed! What do you think? There's a story about tragic lovers, as well. I've asked Sam — the one with the blue hair — to do a mural on that wall, and to design everything. You know, for publicity. And the sign. Local tv are interested.'

The old building makes strange noises. When the wind is in the east, it sounds like a child crying. When it blows from the north, it is more like men fighting. And when it blows from the south, imaginative Alex claims to hear people making love.

'This place would be so much quieter without the chimneys. Doesn't the wind in them sound sad tonight?' Alex asks.

'It always sounds like that when it blows from the west,' says practical Julian. 'It'll carry any boat straight out to sea. Don't think there'll be many slipping their moorings tonight, though.' He puts both arms round Alex and begins a long, if slightly boozy, kiss.

✳ ✳ ✳

In that same room, in the early 1800s, a sailor sat drinking and thinking. His earthenware platter held nothing but a clean chop bone and a few crumbs. He raised his thick tumbler and downed its steaming contents in one noisy gulp. A feeling of generosity warmed him in the same way the food and rum had. 'Who'll drink with me?' he shouted. 'My pockets are full of guineas, and the landlord here mixes very good grog! I'm buying!'

A slim arm curved over his shoulder and a mass of auburn hair fell down beside his face. He could smell clothing stored somewhere damp, female sweat and lavender water. It was a heady mixture and, when he felt the warmth of a kiss beside his mouth, he reached round to discover who this might be.

'Anna!' He looked into her eyes and stiffened. 'What are you doing in this place? I know you, with your eyes the colour of the seas I've sailed! Not the China seas — though I've been there — no, your eyes are the colour of the North Sea on a winter night. That's a sea that men drown in.'

She moved to stand in front of him before she spoke. 'Johnny Martin, you knew me long ago when my blood was as cold as the grey North Sea. You warmed it once, but you went before you knew it. My life has changed. You may have travelled the oceans, visiting the exotic east and the warm south, but I have travelled farther than you without ever leaving this shore. Buy me a drink, and I'll warm your bed and ask for nothing more.'

She sat at the table opposite him, slipped off her shawl and adjusted her bodice so that he saw the moist parting between her swelling breasts and the gentle round curve of her shoulder. In his half-drunk state, he felt he was gazing at the troughs and crests of waves on a southern ocean.

Leaning forward, she picked up his hand. 'Let me read your fortune in your palm. You know I have the gift. The secrets and signs are clear to me.' She turned his right hand over and read the tattoo across the back. 'What's that? Let me see the other!' Seizing his left, she turned that over too and placed his hands side by side.

Together the message was clear: L O V E A N N A.

'Forgive me,' she murmured. 'I did not know. You have travelled too far and I have sunk too low.'

Slipping between the tables and benches, pulling her shawl tightly round her, she was gone before Johnny Martin could get to his feet.

He felt a complete fool.

The girl whose name he carried on his left hand, the side where his heart beat, the girl who had rejected him seven long years ago, Anna had found him on his return to their childhood home while he sat tippling in the Star of the Sea, nerving himself to begin his search for her. But what had become of her?

He banged his fist down, hard, on the rough table so that the tumbler and platter fell to the floor and shattered. The chop bone bounced and skittered out of sight.

The landlord loomed over him. 'Now then, Johnny, you can eat and drink as long as you can pay, but that's it. And let me warn you — Anna's Victor Bulman's now. He'll break your bones if you mess with her.'

Johnny smiled widely, humourlessly. 'So, he's still alive, is he? Victor Bulman, eh? And where will I find him? Counting his greasy shillings in his mother's old clothes shop? Jerking off behind a jakes door?'

'Stay away from him, Johnny. He's mean as mustard, fatal as firedamp. When he blows up, people get hurt. Stay away from him!'

Johnny broke into song, giving the words the rhythm of a sea shanty: 'We'll string him high by his big flat feet /Row away, boys, row away./ And we'll leave him there for the fishes to eat/ At the bottom of the sea till resurrection day/ God can have mercy but none of us may...'

He fell silent for three minutes. When he spoke, his voice was low but clear. 'I can beat Victor Bulman. He's well named. I knew him when he was a fat bully, sneaking to whoever'd listen, full of bullshite. Tell you what, landlord, I'll buy a bottle of rum and a bottle of Malaga red wine from you and I'm going to spend the best night I've ever had!' He thrust two golden guineas on the bar. The landlord stared, bit them, and handed over the liquor.

Johnny picked up the bottles and, one in each hand, turned to face the people in the tavern. 'You're all cowards! You live here, let Bulman tell you what to do, and you won't back me — a man who's seen something of the world — when he tries to rid you of him. You won't drink with me, and you won't save my Anna. What are you? Harbour rats or slimy snails? Not a man among you!'

He did not see the blow coming. A fist thumped him hard, so that he fell back and cracked his head on the bar. 'It sickens me: I come back here and find nothing has changed. A thug rules the place, and the prettiest girl is still in his clutches. I should have stayed in Queenstown with the dusky maidens. Not that they stayed maidens for long...'

He was scanning the dim corners of the smoky room, looking through vision blurred by blood for the face he wanted. He raised his voice and roared: 'Where is she? Where's my girl?'

He swayed, the impact of the blow and the booze taking effect. He knew the black dark of senselessness was about to claim him as he slipped down, down, into a long tunnel towards a crying child. Silhouetted in late afternoon's golden light, she sat — he knew — at the edge of a high cliff.

Peaceful at last, he seated himself beside the child.

'Hello, Anna,' he said. 'Don't let Victor Bulman make you cry. I'm going to run away to sea and make my fortune and when I get home I'll look after you.' He put both arms around her and drew her towards him.

❀ ❀ ❀

It is Bonfire Night, 2020. Julian and Alex stand in the empty dining-room of the Star of the Sea and drink. They have little to say to each other — recent conversations have always been about how they can meet the bills. Behind the bar, the optics are empty though their glasses are full. The wind sobs in the chimneys. Alex, too, is in tears.

'I'm sorry about spending so much on the sign and the mural. I don't know, Ju, I don't know what we can do. We can't borrow any more. We're not eligible for grants. There isn't any casual work I can get.'

'You couldn't even sell your body,' states Julian, mirthlessly. 'Not when you've given it away free so often.'

Alex stares at him, lifts a heavy glass tumbler, drinks half its contents and seems to be about to set it down on the bar. Somehow the movement changes, and Julian feels the glass bang hard against the side of his face and liquid spray over his face. He sees Alex's arm swing towards him again, light flashing on the broken glass that he cannot evade. 'Fuck off!' he roars, then screams as his cheek is sliced open.

❀ ❀ ❀

No one knows what happened next.

An elderly man walking his dog later than usual, because of the fireworks, found Julian unconscious outside the open front door of the poshed-up old Nag's Head. A trail of blood stained the floor from the dining-room all the way to where it had set, pooled under his head, on the new Yorkstone steps.

The only comment made by the WPC summoned to the scene was 'They'll never get that stain out,' but privately she would have liked the Star of the Sea to be a success. 'They'd done it up really tastefully,' she told her husband. 'I don't know where the other one's gone, though. These two weren't on our lists. We think they both had cars, but there was only one parked there. It'll take a while to sort out.' She yawned on her way to bed after her long night. 'Will you get something out of the freezer for tea, love?'

Julian died in the ambulance.

Three days later, when the tide was out, a car with a body inside was spotted at the foot of Bempton Cliffs. There was a photograph of it being winched out on the front page of the next edition of the Monkton Messenger, with a headline of 'New Year's Tragedy'.

❂❂❂

Life in the seaside town of Monkton continues as if nothing much has happened. Another boarded-up building was nothing new, and the story of Julian and Alex has joined that of Johnny and Anna.

The difference is that old town documents and local history groups have recorded and researched the story of Johnny and Anna, but now no one even knows whether Alex was a man or a woman. Does it really matter?

Local mystery, local history.

Susan Perkins

Cornucopia from the Kitchen Sink

Beyond the glint
of the stainless steel sink,
the top of our garden
is a No-Mow-May field,
a voluptuous, bleached blonde,
hedgehog-run and hayfield,
rattling in the scorching sun,

In the middle of it all
the silver birch,
gets giddy,
there's a whisper of breeze
and a green-flutter shimmy.

Nearer the hedge
is the one-tree orchard,
it is only August,
yet a slew of juicy sunsets
needs a sturdy prop,
to hold the sweetness up,
away from the ground,
where the long-bodied beetles,
gather en masse
and begin to creep,
like silent assassins,
to the top of the stems
of the bleached blonde grass.

Janet Philo

Lud's Church

Once upon a post-glacial clock,
a young forest slipped.

Now millstone grit,
still slick with drips,
descends,
in small
uncertain steps
towards a
stone cold
shade.

The devil raked
the mudstone floor,
scarred it with
a single claw
found faults
and fracture planes,
then perched
and watched
bereft,
as lichen's silver antlers grew and
nudged the soft-sprung moss.

Feathered curves of fern
spray the creviced walls
and set the cold clean air alight
with green.

Janet Philo

Lud's Church: A mysterious dark chasm penetrating the Millstone Grit bedrock
above Gradbach in Staffordshire.

In the Kingdom of the Egg

I dreamt myself into an egg
safe within milk-white walls
pinpricked with light

a speck, a chip of garnet
on a pillow of honeyed yolk
I floated in an inland sea

it was not enough

I bloated a rubbery body, lidded eyes
sprouted claws and beak
scribbled scrawny wings

seethed in my cell

gripped in a marble fist
I chipped and chiselled
broke through the dome

staggered into a world of
chickweed and thistles
cloudburst and sunshine

unshelled
        unsafe
                awake

                                        Jenna Plewes

The Bewilderment of Zebedee
Matthew 4: 21-22

Bewildered he watched his beloved sons go,
Not a word was spoken, not even goodbye,
His two boys who loved him, and whom he loved so,
The question that plagued him was just one word, why?

Not a word was spoken, not even goodbye,
Just dropped their nets and walked out of his life,
The question that plagued him was just one word, why?
There'd be tears for sure from Salome, his wife.

Just dropped their nets and walked out of his life,
Neither turned round to glance back again,
There'd be tears for sure from Salome, his wife
As they followed one man to be fishers of men.

Neither turned round to glance back again,
His two boys who loved him, and whom he loved so,
As they followed one man to be fishers of men,
Bewildered he watched his beloved sons go.

Stephen Poole

Pomegranate

Pomegranate
    the golden apple
        of the sun

a bit inflated surely
    for a visit
        to Reg the Veg

on a Sunday morning
    marked by cloud
        and that searing wind

forecasters like to refer to
    as a 'light breeze'
        coming especially in the evening

the time sacred to the guardians
    the Hesperides, whose number
        nobody knows —

Aigle, Erytheia, Hesperia
    perhaps - sunset glow,
        daughters of Nyx,

of endless night
    and nothingness
        warm flesh pip spit

of the pomegranate
    luscious savage
        sharp as Zephyrus

I will put in my bag
    limes from the deepest south
        Iberian oranges

all the tumult of fruit
    but pomegranate, the seeded
        apple, precious beyond

precious, I will leave
    to bathe in the glory
        of sunlight and distant lands

where plunder has not yet come
    and trade winds do not blow —
        to float upon the tree.

David Punter

Scratching her bottom in green ears and a tartan skirt

she stands by the festival tent
   of oldies playing Lonnie Donegan
and the Blues Brothers
   in flagrant adolescent plump

and sky wheels her future
   defiance and bewilderment
am I meant to be here
   here among the sausage rolls

cream teas plastic lager
   alighted from another planet
where all is young and all delight
   growing swirling growing

blue-bright orchestras of sound
   shrunk to needlehead precision
here exactly here but haloed
   as wolf-defeating camp-fires

before she moves aslant away
   and the whole world changes
in elf-slight degree returning
   a Gestalt of glowing empty space

David Punter

Bulbs

I had to be careful when I said bulbs:
she worked in a lamp shop,
and loved her garden.
She shone a light on meanings,
like when as a kid, I saw her eye
fall on the tattered blue coat
of an old woman on the bus
and watched her take in the way
the conductor kept silent
when he took the lady's fare —
a penny short.
I whispered "You're very noticing, mammy."
A dark-haired smile replied "*Observant*, son;
you mean *observant*."
And when the autumn came
she knew where and what to plant,
how winter mask would slip away,
how April sun would cause
greenness to spring up, stems
of red and yellow tulips —
those that greet me now
as I gather them to decorate her grave.

Bill Richardson

spectrums

this bird doesnt bother with
bright colours red and silver hues
and golden sheen are glamorous
on others not for him
       his funny trills plodding beats
       and raging riffs dismantle
       artifice he lapses into silence
       gifts his muteness to us
              his stressors are his siblings
              and the friends he bats away
              there see him hop edgily
              towards the flock then bolt
       he feels the pressure says
       with screwed up eyes how
       life intrudes when all he
       wants is peace that promises
some birds sing a sweeter song
some vibrate with colour our
one trades the red and silver hues
and golden sheen for monochrome

                                        Bill Richardson

Trapped behind the curtain, escape now impossible; velvet pressed forcefully against the stricken victim. A dark shape loomed, growing, as it approached.

Battling in vain against the heavy cloth, like a moth, fluttering in darkness. Then, every ounce of energy sapped, pausing momentarily to regain composure and strength. Unable to cry out, the only sound the battering vibrations of movement — a life in danger.

No-one heard or came to investigate the final crunch.

Stillness permeated the shroud, a corpse yet to be discovered.

The dark shape retreated, no time to leave, no escape possible, act innocent and the deed was soon forgotten, simple. In seconds the killer's focus strayed elsewhere as he wondered what else to do.

His hands toyed idly with a knife on the table next to the window, the strange, twanging noises it made as he poked it into different cracks and materials captivated his attention a while longer. He relaxed.

Noticing the sinister lull, Angela decided to check the front room again. For too long, quiet had persisted, no thumping, clattering, arguing or cries for help.

Caution carried her to the door, she listened, afraid to breathe, motionless — *what was that metallic twanging?* she wondered.

The culprit, stirred at her approaching footsteps.

Angela pressed the door handle downwards, soundless opening, bated breath. The room betrayed nothing. She didn't notice the mark on the window through dazzling shafts of sunlight.

Tom was toying with a knife and this was normal.

As she stepped in, Tom looked up — a picture of guilt but she enquired no further, best not to.

The body remained undiscovered for hours. Only later when Angela went to the window to check who was knocking at the front door would she discover the deed. The black and yellow mark smeared on the window, net curtain and a lifeless outline.

"Tom, have you been killing again?" the enquiry.

"Mummy, why are they called 'squashed fly' biscuits?" the confession.

Julia Rizzi

Libra

Even a spinning top slows
down. But I'm still dizzy
with the spin of it, the vertigo
stomach-jump thrill of it.
And there's no weigh-bridge
to calculate the load, the toll,
the crash-landing. My scales
tip heavy, light, in a mad dance;
sometimes they hover in balance.

Jenny Robb

Nothing's Clear

Our friendship is a house of hoarded clutter; boyfriends, confessions, secrets, office gossip. So tightly packed we no longer see clearly. One spark is all it takes for years to become a clearance. Dust and smoke obscure our shadows, leave each with a different, lonely shape. I don't know where the spark came from.

Phone calls flatline. You don't come round. I hear you're in a pub, or a gig with other friends. You say we can clear the air but the heart of us stops. We both understand the DNR sign.

The severance is an amputation, I feel your phantom presence. I fight the urge to call you, tell you about my daughter's latest adventure in Australia, my fear about her never coming home.

Jenny Robb

Death sat behind me at the opera last night

I recognised him
although he was in mufti,
leaning forward breathing
into my right ear, almost
an intimate caress.
So I fell into conversation
asking *why opera,*
any opera?

He said it was amusing
for him to watch others
doing his job
while the bodies fell
down, got up,
hands on beating hearts
as they bowed solemnly
to rapturous applause.

O heroic gesture!
O descanted emotion!
O narrative of death
so unlike the usual
stagger to the Styx,
the boat-ride to oblivion,
the crumbling disbelief
in me and my bony finger.

It's a pleasure he said
to sit here in penumbra
listening to the breathing
of singers and instruments,
the nervous audience
sensing entitlement
might be wrenched away
after the interval bar.

He blew a strand of hair
across my eyes.
Everything went dark

briefly, I thought it over —
before the lights came up
and I realised it wasn't.
We gathered our effects,
our scarves, our phones.

We'll be in touch he said
I've got your number.

Gillie Robic

O

February 2022

What's the weight of a carrier bag, a bin-bag of clothes?
a Spiderman toy
the press of a tank that has carved up the lawn
these suitcases we hold
what pasts they destroy
o my girl o my boy?

What's brighter than light and soaks through the dawn?
makes paving slabs tremble
what opens the doll's houses all down the street
bricks and wallpaper torn
each room disassembled
o my girl o my boy?

What did you hold on to?
The straps of a rucksack
the hand of my daughter, the voice of my neighbour
the song I sang back to
as fear froze my throat in a rocket attack
o my girl o my boy

Whose are these footsteps?
past park and the square
what life do they come from
what goodbyes neglect?
The dolls wait in their cupboards, they stare and they stare
o my girl, o my boy

This is the train but where is the station?
it severs all meaning
to look at each other —
the soup kitchen steams and ladles its ration
a dream wakes up screaming
o my girl o my boy

Graeme Ryan

St Paul of Mariupol

A Ukrainian soldier faces himself in the mirror

I faced the court of who I was and heard the charges read out:

that I was an oligarch cruising my seas of privilege,
that I drilled armies of opinion, dug trenches for my ignorance,

squandered nights and dawns with online poker
and a brimful of shots, exulted in the codes of my tribe,

blocked my wife's path with a look and a shoulder-barge
as she bundled my dirty laundry into the machine.

I'd chuck small change into a beggar's cap for the virtue-rush,
fling dog-mess over the fence to fuel the neighbour's rage,

ride my mower hard over the moral high ground.
You're not the man I — she said. I took it out on the children,

could justify every special operation in the smoke-filled hours.

The judgement descended.
          I shivered in the dock.
                    The judge spat me out like a fly.

I was sent down, chained to a wall.

One day a samizdat of sunlight found me:
'Dumb fool, you have done your time.' My hair froze.

'There is some good in you and this shoot will grow.
This much is real: all you have now is the breath of your body

and the naked truth of it. Can fear be burnt away?
What if this vapour were just mist over the roofs one summer?

When the heat-seeking missile butchers the tower-block
know that you did all a human being can do. Stripped yourself

down to the bare bones, made a deal with your self-pity,
fought for life in this upturned air. Rest a while,

your wife and kids have not forgotten you. Nothing stops the time
when the soul expands beyond a million crimes and apparitions,

the wicked ones turn to ghosts and the bullets melt.
Truth fires its truth from the chambers of the heart —

makes you a being of light in these bunkered ruins.'

Graeme Ryan

The Virgin of Milk and Alphabets

This is the story told to me as I sat in my grandma Caterina's arms as a baby, as a *ragazza* — then told again as a teen, as a young adult. The story is about two girls leaving an island she called Persephone's Island (Sicily), who would be orphaned by their daddy, raised by their mama, work in a factory, and then be married in an arrangement — Caterina to Pa Tony and Anna to Seguti.

I have painted this story with imagery of blue waters of my own dreams. I have painted a story with a liberal brush in my need to understand my little grandma Caterina who would conceive and deliver my father; to understand myself and how this story affects my choices.

Did Caterina's mother, my great grandma, say to her two daughters, "Today you will meet your future husbands, pointing to the wardrobe where the two Sunday dresses delegated for Sunday Mass and newly washed and pressed, hung? Their mother would have said, "*Vai*. Go put them on. We won't be late for the arrangement." The sisters might have looked at each other, speaking with their eyes, knowing something was up, dressing in their best frocks, the ones with gardenias on a cream colored background. Maybe blue and pink roses? Or a navy blue? Hopefully not black.

What went on in their minds? Two sisters, nineteen and twenty, dressing for the arrangement their mother had made; two sisters bathing quickly in water drawn from boiled water in a pan mixed with cold. Did they rebel? Look at each other crooked? Maybe they felt excited, maybe scared. You might see them taking time, stalling with the buttons of the navy blue Sunday dresses. You might see them primping their hair. Maybe they had braids and Caterina would wind them around her head the way the actors at the Bowery did or wear them in long pigtails down her back. You might feel the excitement as palpable — two young women going to the arrangement. Will there be one man who will choose one of them — leaving the other left to another fate, separating them?

In my painting I see them in a new parlor, standing shoulder to shoulder, looking deeply into each others' eyes, and then back and forth to their mother. With tight lips they wait, look around the room for signals as to what's going on. The parlor, not so shabby as theirs — the couch covered in plastic, a chair soft with full arms, a funny shaped lamp whose ceramic base had a little cherubs dancing around it. They wait, maybe holding their breath, holding hands.

The time passes slowly. They hear voices, bass voices, rumbling voices in the old language behind the door of the room; they hear footsteps and their insides shake. They look at each other, knowing nothing will be the same after the game in this parlor, where voices behind closed doors resound — men's voices. The sisters take each other's hand, worrying they will be separated. Two sisters, who traveled across the sea as little girls, live their karma now. Barely out of their teens they stand in front of the threshold of some arrangement with the deep voices getting closer. Then silence.

Hand-in-hand they look at each other in time that seems to stand still. Silence. The knob slowly turns. The door squeaks open. They watch. They hold their breaths as the palms of their hands sweat into each others, making wet heat. They watch two men, one short and one tall, come through the door. The taller one bends his head under the doorway to enter. Two young men face them, dressed in scruffy suit jackets with worn-out patches at the elbow. Leather shoes look too tight, too uncomfortable, too big, too brown.

Now a woman comes into the room — a well-dressed woman unlike the others. She wears a crepe dress with the white lace collar and a black hat with a stiff feather. Her shoes are thick heeled in the fashion of the day like the ones at the Jordan Marsh store. She's different from Caterina and her sister. She speaks English perfectly well like the matron in the factory where the sisters learned their English. She stands there as if she's cracking a whip, examining each sister up-and-down, quickly assessing. Then like the factory master she speaks.

"You will go with him," she says to Caterina, pointing to the tall one.

Would nineteen year-old Caterina later wonder about how fate played a part in the matron's decision that she would marry the taller brother who would live to be seventy-seven while Anna would marry the shorter one who'll die, making her a widow with babies. Would Caterina know the good strong man would refuse to speak a word of English all those fifty plus years of marriage? Would she curse the fate which brought her to the marriage bed with a man who wore worn-out leather shoes — more comfortable in gray workers clothes, wooly socks and a flannel shirt, wondering how she had ended up with him — the man who would be the father of her children

I paint a picture of a young woman with a distant gaze looking into Pa Tony's blue eyes, seeing the deep blue from which she came — the sea and the blue horizon where the Mediterranean meets an azure sky. With this image her world opens wide, creating space from head to toe, allowing her to stretch forward and back and forward again with an awareness that the story of her life *came from afar before stones were born.* Perhaps she feels blessed like the Virgin Mary when she first learns she'll have a child who will be a savior.

Caterina never imagines her destiny as her eyes meet his hand reaching out to touch hers. A man's hand with fingers long and strong caress hers, releasing her hunger for connection. Without words he speaks to her, reaching her heart pounding like a drum in her chest. And for a moment she does not see the others in the room. She does not know what they notice for she only hears the song of drums beating in her chest. His touch calls her to those blue eyes — windows open a craving inside her.

You might think she's in a trance the way she stares at his eyes. You might think she's crazy, believing these eyes speak; that his touch opens up the sky and tells her of things past and future. You might think she's losing herself with a silent blue-eyed man standing before her. If you can't see the sea and the past in him, you might think Caterina has disappeared. You can't feel her terrible longing for her father.

She moves a step closer to him and then takes a step away for his energy courses through her veins. Tony looks down and stares at his hands, cupping hers. While saliva, puddles in her mouth, she tastes lilac flowers and musk. She wonders how long she has been staring at this tall man with strong hands and blue eyes who doesn't speak to her with words.

But his hands have words. They say, "Hold me. See me. Stand by me." They say, "I am strong and will protect you. They tell her that they will build cities. They say. "All I need is you." The hands become the vehicle for his communication. She takes this hand and brings it to her face and let's the fingers roam around her soft skin, still with baby fuzz. His fingers make small circles on her cheeks — cheeks that have not been caressed since she was a little girl; hands that might comfort her.

Caterina remembers her daddy's hands when they held her on the swaying ship crossing the Atlantic Ocean. Sometimes they would reach out to help her manage the big steps of the boat, "*Vieni qui,* come here," he said, taking her hands in his. Hands that held onto the rail of the ship as it heaved her to and fro. Yes, her daddy's hands were strong but they had disappeared soon after they landed in America, soon after they found the shelter in the crowded tenements of the North End of Boston; hands that carried their few bags up the many flights to the attic apartment became hands that gestured to Mama when he told her, "*Arriverderci.* Goodbye, I'm leaving. I'm done! I'm going back to Sicily." Hands that lifted her high to the sky before he left and never came back.

She dreamed of her daddy every night. She dreamed he would return, send a message of his whereabouts, his well-being. But nothing! No word from him. She imagined he'd been in danger on that rolling ship, that he had rolled away into that big sea and that in some way it had been her fault.

Her mama would have wondered, "What will I do? How? Two young children?" *Un'amica* might have assured her she would help with the little girls; that they could work in the factory, too, sorting and someday sewing

And so once upon a time a little girl would learn that her story was nothing but questions made of the words of the new language. She would learn to read and write; she was going to speak English and Italian, even Yiddish; she would become self-educated. *The stones had been cast long before she was born.*

How Tony's eyes and hands fit into her story, she doesn't know. What she knows is that she will manage this annunciation as the Virgin Mary did when she learned she would have a son who would be a savior. What she does not know is that the sacrifice she makes of giving up her independence in favor of his protective hands, is her futile attempt to have the hands of her father who long ago abandoned her.

She does not know that she can never retrieve her father.

She cannot know this love is a trap and not a love that allows a girl to fly high, to be anything, to go anywhere. In exchange for a dream of a hand and protection, she will nurture his strong hands until they became arthritic. She cannot know that Tony would never speak a word of English till the day he died; she cannot know she would never be a reader and writer. She cannot know she would give her milk to Tony as if he were her son and not her husband.

She cannot know that Tony would curse their son born with a club foot, a son who would study and become a lawyer and not work with his hands and feet as a laborer; she cannot know that she would hold a grand baby, me, in her arms and whisper alphabets — ah, bee, chee, dee, ehf, feh, gee, A-B-C-D-E-F-G in her ears so that she could write her gramma's story. She cannot know that she would be the milk of the family, nursing her husband for fifty years, nursing their son and then the girl too, feeding her alphabets and breads and pizzas and pastas.

She would never know that she was the virgin of milk and alphabets.

Barbara Sapienza

Snapshots taken at the Zoo

Perhaps they sensed it coming
like cows do with an approaching storm.
But I hope not.

They were probably used to the whines of sirens
but not the drone of planes overhead
or the whistle of falling bombs.

As their enclosure collapsed around them
the elephants screamed,
a manic, experimental choral work.

A gibbon looked bemused
as its paws were sheared off
like a thief from the Middle Ages.

Pressed down by the weight of falling debris,
a hippopotamus sank into its pool,
a grey battleship holed below the waterline.

Their keepers pointed guns at the lions
like a firing squad taking aim
at members of their own family.

Stiff-legged like a circus performer on stilts,
a giraffe galloped from the fires of Dresden,
searching for some sort of freedom.

Dave Smith

V for Vincent

She was away when they had learnt
about Antarctica and The Arctic
but she already knew about penguins and stuff.
She was glad that she was back for Van Gogh though.

Her sentence was so good that Miss
made the rest of the class copy it out.
"I see a vase full of cheerful flowers
like little suns on stems."
She was going to write sticks
but she remembered the proper word just in time.

She was sorry that Vincent was dead
because she wanted to teach him
how to write a proper V and
ask him to paint a unicorn for her.

So she painted one herself
and was particularly pleased with its horn.
Miss had told them that
only good people went to Heaven.
Surely Vincent would be there
because his paintings made people happy.

She looked up into the sky and
whispered "Vincent", having been told
God didn't listen to shouts.

She hoped that Vincent would
stop painting for a minute,
look down and smile,
although if you were in Heaven
you would probably be smiling all of the time.

Dave Smith

Modelling for Spencer Tunick

You are sun-grazed cobbles
  as you lie close
in rows of four and five
  pale hairs on your folded arms
filling the space between
  with backbones in line
shoulders buttocks
  and hips that sway slightly
if your eyes glance sideways
  you feel alive at
five in the morning
  bodies as still as the dawn chill
when the camera shutter clicks and whirrs
  on a street of human spines
flowing to the Tyne.

Kate Swann

The Puddings

Mr Devine's Vagina is in the powder room and the lawyers are debating if she will be wanting a pudding. *I am not allowed to make decisions for her*, Mr Devine protests. *Let's wait for her.*

Vincenza says, *It's completely ridiculous to even suggest that she will be saying yes to a pudding* and is already totting up the bill.

On Mr Devine's Vagina's powder room re-emergence, Vincenza holds her head back, laughs and says provocatively, *We have concluded that you are highly unlikely to be saying yes to a pudding.*

Mr Devine's Vagina inhales, stares long and hard at her boyfriend, then startles the table with an unexpected toot, *You know, I think I WILL have a pudding. In fact, I'll have two, we will share them all together with Theo.* Mr Devine's 17-year-old instantly beams at the idea of being allowed to have pudding.

There are a variety of groans amongst the others at the table and the menu appears from an excited waitress and Mr Devine's Vagina *Um's* and *Ah's* endlessly about the banana blancmange and lemon curd cheesecake options. The deliberation is particularly unnecessary as she can't even have the 3rd option, the chocolate volcano, as she is highly allergic — if she has one whiff of a chocolate, she will consume an entire box and then seek out more chocolates, this pattern often lasting weeks at a time, ending only on physical restraint.

The puddings take 20 minutes to arrive. In the meantime, Mr Devine's Vagina tells me about how they met in a café and how she refused to go on a date with him but he had insisted she take his number. Then out of the blue, one morning when she was lying in bed bored a year later, battery depleted, recharging, she scrolled through ALL the names in her phone and on arriving at his remembered THAT MAN who once fancied her, YES, fancied HER, and decided to text him and he immediately replied and here they are a year later. But she says that there are many, many, many problems and she says she would love to take me aside and discuss ALL of their personal problems with me away from the others as they are VERY private indeed.

Mr Devine, oblivious to the nature of this talk and deep in conversation about tax matters with the lawyers, frolics and gropes with her under the table. There is a disturbing amount of reciprocal rubbing and fumbling with her giggling as we chat and I try to steer things to less awkward topics and wish I had a better handle on tax and economic policy.

The puddings arrive — 2 spoons, one for Theo and one for Mr Devine who is now vigorously spooning his Vagina. Theo's pudding is somehow in the mix too and they all devour them with utter delight, slurping greedily. I am asked if I would like to join the feeding frenzy and wonder with the lack of spoons if this would mean my being passively spoon fed by Mr Devine, a gaping mouth in turn with his Vagina. I decline to participate fearful of being sucked into the abyss of this blancmange orgy.

I sip my English Breakfast tea.

Eleanor Jane Turner

Sudan

after gentle rain and birth
warm air lifts the lapwing's cry
and the lamb

so small
hangs to his mother's teat
unknowing this heaven in which he is born

is a fleeting spring
a lick of honey

whilst overhead the magpies circle
pick off after-birth
like snipers smell blood

the ewe retreats
nudges her new-born
to the border beside

blackthorn blossom
a field's stone wall
insurmountable without flight

imagine wings in their eyes
gunfire closing in

Julia Usman

Swan

For beauty with sorrow is a burden hard to be borne — Walter de la Mare

Regal, she ripples diagonal across the lake
arcs the soft curve of her neck —
an orchid flower on a stem

she is teaching me a second language —
words for light, grace, forgiveness
insists I follow as she haunts the dusk

wears her widowhood in the black of her eyes

I do not see her weep
but note the blank space
between her body and the shore

her solitary journey stirs grief

I imagine her whispering his name - and
when the willows steal her, all she leaves behind
is the moon paused on the surface of the water

Julia Usman

Flight into Egypt

Running down the lean days,
west on the A13 from Tilbury
to the 406 through Grays,
at the turn after Christmas
when time looks both ways

and me a sole trader, working
the overnighters at low rates
on Red Diesel with trade thin
the Tach' 'adjusted' for the Bill,
to keep it sweet, my credit clean,

and a bastard northerly's blowing
sleet then rain then sleet again
black slush and the rig swerving,
so I turn in at Scrutton's Farm,
off road for the truckers' canteen.

You see it happen all the time:
an Artic' at two in the morning
swung away from the halogen,
doors open and you see them,
sky divers falling out in line

usually men, perhaps with a plan
thin as you like, hard, freezing
and it's a scene from Stalag 17
scattering, where to unknown;
but this time, a woman with a man

and she's clutching something,
hard to her ribs, wrapped tight
in blankets warm under her coat
and they're pleading, the driver
threatening, more money passing.

Sleet becomes a driven snow
and I'm by the tea stand thinking,
about all this coming in, our Sharon
with her baby and no job or housing,
what all of it will mean for them,

and I'm thinking, this couple driven,
how if I was them I'd do the same,
how they might be a new beginning,
or an ending of everything I know,
or just rocks thrown in a river's flow

and I know this cold could kill them
clamped tight in each other's arms;
do I leave them to it, to become
what the streets will make of them,
or open up my cab — call them in?

Christiaan Van Bussel

Paranoia is a beautiful thing

The dollhouse of your mind
is constantly ransacked
behind your back. Appointment
dates are turned into coleslaw.
Birthdays are fed to a wandering lion.
Dinner dates spin like plates
on the tongue of a blind contortionist.
Faces of those closest to you
are lost in a bowl of keys colder
than gravestones. Social media
is a hazy mirage. Every password
is a meaningless self-portrait.
You'd blame stress, family curses,
a history of eccentricity, artistic
tendencies, and the wrong medication,
but none of those things exist in your life.
The crow who always says your name
is keeping quiet, won't drop any hints,
while your phone performs another act
of subliminal messaging.

Christian Ward

Those who witness, gagged by so much hot air

You have come this far, through the trees and
          fire, you, watching over this earth, already
walked along sharp-edged borders,
          saw youth riddled by the hail and, let into the
secret too early, fade into the storm.

Death, hunger, wars, so many chapters of a book
          of inexhaustible content.

Is this not another landscape now, a semblance
          that looms out of nightfall,
a divided-up worn-out land-living world of passers-by whose
          memory is sieve-like, no dreams left, at the
end of the road.

Patrick Williamson

Lead City

Smiler stepped out, slowly, on to the cracked paving stones outside the front gate, which was missing. Grass had sprung up and withered between the pavement cracks and in the gutters by the kerbside. The dust he kicked up made him cough something unspeakable, which he spat between his feet. He ambled towards the station, by the back road into the subway, where it was cool, where bindweed choked the peeling railings. His slow pace was unusual for someone so young, but already he carried a gaunt, skeletal frame. He looked up towards the distant tall office blocks in the financial district.

'Lead city,' he muttered, 'The day intense, a heavy jelly hanging in the atmosphere.'

He entered the subway and sat down on his usual pitch.

'Spare 'ny CHANGE please, sir, madam?'

The subway smelt of piss, among other things. There was something sticky but invisible on one or two of his fingers. Then three or four as he struggled to wipe it on his jeans.

Smiler smiled when the money dropped into his (used) plastic cup. Smiler smiled when the money missed it. Smiler smiled when he had to trap rolling money with his foot. Smiler smiled when there was no money. Smiler did not smile when there was no one passing. Sometimes, Smiler wanted to kill someone. Not anyone in particular, just someone.

After the morning rush, around ten, people stopped coming. After ten 'o clock, trains arrived every half hour, substantially empty, and left the same. Smiler crossed the road to the stall. Just at the right time. No customers for a bit, the stall man bored. Time to dump the incredible assortment of coppers, five pence pieces, foreign coins and tokens, on to the counter.

The stall man winced. The money already smelled of Smiler's damp and mouldy squat. After examining the pile, he handed Smiler a few pound coins from the till, then swept the heap of shrapnel away in exchange for burger, chips and tea.

'All right Smiler?'

'Yeh.'

There was another smell, behind Smiler. Perfume.

'All right love?'

'Dad, have you got a minute?'

Father and daughter drew away far enough for a private conversation.

'The stall man's beautiful daughter,' Smiler muttered.

Smiler ate. The expanded foam burger case squeaked and bristled — at first accidentally — as his hands and mouth moved, making him wince. Then the sounds became louder and more experimental. The woman broke off her quiet conversation. Her hurt eyes implored silence. Smiler smiled and squeaked all the more.

'Smiler,' the Stall Man grimaced.

'Yeh?'

'Shut the fuck up.'

Smiler withdrew, a chip tumbled on to the counter. He returned to his pitch and sat on his coat.

'Bastard!' he muttered. 'Snotty Bastard'.

He picked up a few words of the conversation:

'Don't worry about Scott Dad... he doesn't know where I live now...'

'If he shows his face here......if he try's anything .... just let me know....'

The chips were gone. Smiler picked up his coat, binned the rubbish and went up on to the platform. There was no point in being there again until six, there were school kids in the afternoon, but they just took the piss and nicked his cup.

They didn't care about tickets on the stations. The barriers were left open. The Gestapo only came at rush hours. Even then they couldn't do much. Even their phones were crap at checking someone with no address. It was the shit they gave him he didn't like. So, he rode free to the next station, where the bloke in the shop gave him a box of out-of-date food for a couple of quid.

'Smiler's daily triangle,' he said, 'home — work — shopping.'

Back home, he carried the box to the kitchen and put the stuff that needed it in the fridge. He drew his sleeping bag over him on the old settee and crashed till five. The others were all still out when he woke up and the food was as he had left it.

Monday, and it was the morning rush again, there were dead leaves and chip papers blowing down the stairs from the platform.

Smiler was phased by the young man in the pin-striped suit. All the others carried their props — bags, cases, mobiles, cigarettes. But he carried nothing and he walked with his fists clenched.

'Spare 'ny small CHANGE Sir?'

The clenched fists did not unclench.

'Dust and sunshine,' Smiler observed, when he was past, 'as the people start their day — the hewers of wood and the clenchers of fists."

Clencher did not go up the stairs. He sidled into obscurity in the corner of the blind end of the subway, waiting.

Clattering heels, perfume. The Stall Man's Daughter. Her own pin-striped suit, briefcase. She didn't see Clencher and pretended not to see Smiler.

'Spare 'ny small CHANGE Madam?'

Only, when she was about to turn to the steps —

'Stephanie!'

She turned, smiling business charm. The smile evaporated as she recognised him.

'Scott.'

'So you're not coming back to me,' he blurted.

She slowly shook her head, meeting his eyes.

'Come back,' he pleaded.

'Where?'

'Steph….'

'I've got nothing to say to you if you're going to be like this.' She started up the stairs. He waited, clenching, then ran after her.

Smiler smiled.

It was rare that Police Community Support entered the subway. Police Community Support did not make Smiler smile. He smiled even less at the sight of special constables, who were even more short of anything to do. But Police Community Support, who always came in twos, were coming along by the railings.

He decided to move before they decided to move him. The barriers were open, no ticket inspectors. He walked up the stairs and on to the platform. They did not follow. Surprised, Smiler deduced that they had come to milk Stall Man of gossip.

The cup in one hand, the squeaky chip box in the other, Smiler arrived on the platform. It was the busiest time. The commuters stood still, dense behind the yellow line. Except for Scott, pacing back and forth agitated, on the wrong side of it. Smiler saw Stephanie looking uncomfortable, hoping Scott would not see her. The announcement came. 'Would — CUSTOMERS — please stand away from the edge of platform one, the next train at this platform is not stopping at this station.'

Smiler walked happily on the wrong side of the yellow line 'Spare any CHANGE?'

Scott was coming towards him. Their paths met exactly in front of Stephanie.

Somehow as Scott and Smiler passed each other, the cup of money fell from Smiler's hand and coins rolled on the platform. For an instant there was pure anger on Smiler's face in place of the smile. Somehow, a chip fell from his other, squeaky container. Scott's leading foot met it, slipped, and he stumbled. He grabbed the nearest person who was Stephanie,

'Get off me!' She shouted, 'leave me alone!' She struggled.

Scott, completely unbalanced tried to steady them both. She being lighter, swung round, one foot over the platform edge. They seemed to dance for an instant, then he slipped back on to the platform. He didn't fall, he stumbled, into Stephanie. She hovered still for ever, then, gaining momentum, she floundered down on to the track with a scream. People gasped as they realised the rails were hissing and the train was already at the platform end. The train brakes squealed ineffectually. A long, long, sound of surf, and then screeches, as it came to a halt far too late, far too far off.

'You bastard!'

'You pushed her!'

Scott was blocked by the crowd. Smiler turned back and walked down the stairs. He would travel faster than the news.

Stall Man was cleaning his counter. 'All right Smiler?'

'Yeh.'

'What's happening up there?'

'Dunno.'

Smiler bought chips and began to rhythmically stroke the squeaking wrappings against each other. He was still smiling and stroking and squeaking when the flashing blue lights arrived. He smiled and stroked and squeaked as Stall Man turned grey with shock at what the police told him.

'I saw it all,' Smiler announced.

The policeman looked Smiler up and down.

'Look we are busy. GO AWAY.'

'Have you got a job in the police? I need a job. I'm good at seeing things.'

The second policeman looked up from his phone. 'You heard him, we don't care what you saw. GO AWAY or you'll end up in the Nick.'

'I expect you can tell,' Smiler looked the stall holder in the eye as he left, 'that I've got leadership in me'. He decided he didn't like his pitch at the station. He would walk to the market. Better hours, more shopping later in the mornings, no need to get up early.

'Lead City,' Smiler muttered, 'the silent scream of the commuter as she flounders down on to the tracks. Spare 'ny CHANGE sir.'

Keith Willson

117

Dog

Every night I pray to Dog and each night she comes and sits on the cold concrete outside my door. I watch her through the thick Perspex, and she watches me. I whisper to her and say "I'm sorry I can't let you in" but she understands. I know she is there to guard me, to protect me and them, but they don't seem to care or even see her. Sometimes, it's like its only me and Dog, staring at each other through the transparent divide. I can't feed her, all my meals are posted to me by silent guards, though she doesn't seem to mind. There she sits for hours, watching. On occasion, I have heard her whimper like a beaten puppy, or howl in the early hours like a banished wolf. Yet no-one else hears or stirs. Just Dog and me. She speaks for me because I have lost my language, my words are slurred. I am inebriated on my own company, drunk on solitude. I can bang the glass, Morse Code SOS, but that rarely ends well. So, Dog and I read each other's minds, eye to eye, tooth to tooth. I have seen her snarl, saliva spotting the wall. She is not always placid; she keeps me in my pen. Dog is obedient but, like me, she will never leave here no matter what she does. She broods. I can sense a moonlit night because she dozes and dreams, and I can smell the blood. For one hour every day I am let out, and she trots beside me as I circumnavigate the yard. She is grateful for the exercise, but I worry it isn't enough, that she will fade away and lose her senses and her wild voice. There is nothing for either of us to do but eat and sleep and walk and pray. And wait. And observe each other through the bullet-proof glass. In the past, I have pleaded for concessions — a TV, human company, a budgie — but have been refused on every count. It is too dangerous. I am too dangerous. I am a ticking time-bomb, a conundrum, a mine secreted beneath the earth; my soul rotting until Dog arrived to save me. I see her now, her nose pressed against the smeared Perspex, alert, gazing at me. She will not let me pass because she knows I will kill again, and I am grateful.

Charlotte Wilson

Pondlife

Weight is critical, and tension —
Feather-light, the skater propels on waves,
Buoyed by blind faith and captive air,
Striding across the algae-mottled trampoline
Like an adolescent, newly drunk on summer,
Trusting their bulk to divine cohesion
And the brave assumption
That nothing treacherous lurks beneath.

Charlotte Wilson

About the Contributors

Edward Alport - a retired teacher and proud Essex Boy - occupies his time as a poet, gardener and writer. He has had poetry published in a variety of webzines and magazines and BBC Radio.

Phil Askham was an academic writer of text books, research papers and professional magazine articles. Upon retirement in 2012, Phil took up writing poetry as therapy.

John Atkinson's writing tries to capture the sound and images of people as they live their lives. Previously published in international magazines and a playwright; he hails from Wexford, Ireland.

Alex M Barry is a Bristol-based architect with a love of poetry. First prize Coverstory books 2022 poetry competition. Numerous poems played on BBC Radio Bristol's "Upload" with Adam Crowther.

Actively writing and publishing poetry since 2011, Clare M Bercot Zwerling lives in Northern California and is a member of the Writers of the Mendocino Coast.

Margaret Beston is the author of two collections: *Long Reach River*; *Timepiece*, a pamphlet, *When the Ground Crashed Upwards* and founder of Roundel in Tonbridge.

Ama Bolton lives in Somerset with a sculptor and a hen. An e-chapbook *Nines* is forthcoming from Snapshot Press.

James Callan lives on the Kāpiti Coast, New Zealand. His writing has appeared in *Carte Blanche, Bridge Eight, White Wall Review, Mystery Tribune*, and elsewhere.

Joseph Chaplain is a writer who lives in the Peak District. So far, his work has appeared in *New Contexts* (1 & 2), *The Rebis*, and Crystal Peak's *Dark Folklore* anthology.

Landscape, nature, weather, man's destruction, local history & his farm all inspire Andrew Collinson. *Northern Counties Collection, Pendle War Poetry, Networds* & *Plumb Tree Tavern* all exhibit his work.

Linda M. Crate (she/her) is a Pennsylvanian writer. She has twelve published chapbooks, and her debut photography collection was published April 2023.

Kerry Derbishire has always lived in Cumbria, a landscape that inspires her writing. She's published widely and has three collections, two pamphlets, and a third due in 2024.

Brian Docherty is a Glasgow-Irish post-Beat poet, 8 books, most recently *Only in St. Leonards - A Year on the Marina* (2017), *Blue to the Edge* (2020), *The View From the Villa Delirium* (2021).

Philip Dunkerley is active in poetic circles in South Lincolnshire, where he lives. His poems quite often sneak past editors, and he loves inflicting them on all-comers at open mic events.

A Londoner, Polly East taught in secondary schools while raising her children. Now living in Brighton, she has more time to fine tune her writing. She has been long listed for the National Poetry Competition.

John Edwards lives and writes in Spain. Passionate on wildlife issues and believes in poetic protest. Politics and injustice he will comment on.

Poetry hijacked Angela Ellis in Lockdown. She explores the elasticity of form, imagery and time. Art and nature often feature in her work. She lives in Devon.

Adele Evershed has been nominated for Best of the Net and The Pushcart Prize. Her two poetry chapbooks were published by Finishing line Press and Bottlecap Press. Find her at https://www.thelithag.com.

Lara Frankena's poems have appeared in publications such as *Poetry News*, *Oxford Poetry* and *Magma* and were longlisted for the Erbacce Prize in 2021, 2022 and 2023. She lives in London.

Jim Friedman is a member of the Derby Poetry Stanza. He had his first collection of poems published in 2022. He is working on a second collection.

Lindsay Fursland is a former teacher, living in Cambridge. He is the Poetry Society's Stanza rep in the city, leading monthly workshops, where he also helps to host regular open mic poetry events.

Siobhan Gifford lives in the shade of the North York Moors which, along with her family, often haunt the ley lines of her poems. Recent work has appeared in two anthologies from White Rose Bards.

Ian Gouge is a writer of both fiction and poetry. In 2023 he performed his long poem *Crash* at the Ripon Theatre Festival. His latest fiction is *Tilt, Once Significant Others*, and the short story collection *An Irregular Piece of Sky*.

Diana Hills is retired and started to write poetry recently following a life changing event. She performs poems at various East Sussex pubs, as short and funny as possible.

Ben Hramiak is an author with a Bachelor's Honours in English Literature and Creative Writing. He is currently writing a historical fiction novel set in feudal Japan.

Tom Larner is an archivist based in Bedfordshire. He has been published in New Contexts 4, and magazines such as Crank, Canon, Poetry Cove and The Littoral.

S.J. Litherland lives in Durham. Her eighth collection *Marginal Future* is due from Smokestack in 2024. She has two Northern Writers' Awards, and two National Poetry Comp Commendations.

Ann Logan's retirement rekindled her love of reading and writing poetry. A Devon-dwelling Canadian/British science and politics nerd with so much to write about.

Carmina Masoliver has shared her poetry on page and stage for over a decade; her book *Circles* is published by Burning Eye Books, taking place on the tube.

Caroline Matusiak as published in early years education. A contributor to the Rumbold Report. She enjoys wild swimming, hiking and open mic nights.

Mark Mayes enjoys writing poems, stories, and songs, as well as some non-fiction.

Penny McCarthy has published poems in various journals; a pamphlet of poems set in France, *The Stealing Shadow*; and books and articles on Shakespeare and the Sidney circle.

Emmaline O'Dowd lives in Derby, and has had work in a range of magazines, including *Orbis, Acumen, Popshot* and *Pennine Platform*.

Alfie Ormsbee is an English teacher from Royal Oak, MI. He has been published by Coverstory Books, Allegory Ridge, Quillkeeper's Press, and High Shelf Press.

Carol Park Carol Park teaches ESL. For joy she writes, hikes, reads, and volunteers in a jail. She studied writing with Seattle Pacific University. Find links to her fiction and poetry at www.CarolPark.us.

Jonty Pennington-Twist's work has been published in several anthologies. He has recently written a commissioned piece to mark the RNLI's 200th anniversary.

Susan Perkins writes stories and poems for her family, friends and writing group, after learning the basics when she worked in publishing and then in teaching.

Based in Ashbourne, Janet Philo has two solo pamphlets, and work in anthologies and online. She enjoys mixing spoken poetry with her husband's guitar music.

Jenna Plewes loves collies, and wild places. She's selling her latest collection *A Lick of Loose Threads*, published 2023, in aid of MSF. Find her on FaceBook and Poetry PF

Stephen Poole is a retired policeman. His poems have appeared in *The Ekphrastic Review, Poetry on the Lake*, and *LPP Magazine. New Contexts: 5* is the eighth anthology to publish his work.

David Punter is a poet and academic. He has published nine collections, the most recent of which are *Those Other Fields* (Palewell, 2020), *Stranger* (Cinnamon, 2021) and *Ship's Log* (2022).

Bill Richardson had poems published in, inter alia, *The Stony Thursday Book, Orbis, The Orchards, Skylight 47, 14, The High Window*, and the *Fish Anthology*.

Julia Rizzi has published short stories, features, poetry, simple recipes and is a member of Hertford Writers' Circle. Find her at https://www.linkedin.com/in/julia-rizzi/

Jenny Robb, from Liverpool, is widely published in magazines and anthologies. Her debut collection, *The Doll's Hospital* (Yaffle Press) was published in 2022.

Gillie Robic was born in India. Pamphlet: *Open Skies* in aid of Ukraine; books: *Swimming Through Marble* and *Lightfalls* (all Live Canon). A third due in November.

Graeme Ryan, Poet, playwright, naturalist, lives between Exmoor and the Quantocks, member of Somerset's Fire River Poets. His *Valley of the Kings* was published in 2022.

Barbara Sapienza - inspired by granddaughters - writes *Anchor Out* (2017), *The Laundress* (2020), *The Girl in the White Cape* (2023). She dances, paints and does tai chi.

Dave Smith's debut collection, *Standing Alone, Leaning Against*, was published in 2022 by Coverstory books.

Kate Swann's first poetry collection, *Ripples Beyond the Pool*, was published in 2019 by Coverstory Books. She has subsequently published a gritty, family biography, *Phyll to her Friends*.

Eleanor Jane Turner is happiest when swimming. She enjoys the outdoors, especially remote Scotland. She presents her creative writing at the Forest Hill Stanza.

Julia Usman published her first prose work *A Little Country* with Coverstory books in the autumn of 2022, following a poetry collection *She who sings is not always happy* in 2021.

Christiaan Van Bussel is retired and live in East London. He has always written poetry and was a prize winner in the 1983 National Poetry Competition.

Christian Ward is a UK-based writer who has recently appeared in the *Rappahannock Review*, *South Florida Poetry Journal*, *Full House Literary*, and *Double Speak*.

Patrick Williamson is a poet and translator. His latest collection is *Here and Now* (Cyberwit.net). He is a member of editorial board of The Antonym.

Keith Wilson lives in East Sussex where he performs his songs and poems. He is currently completing an OU MA in Creative Writing.

Charlotte Wilson writes in Ripon, North Yorkshire, about nature, spirituality and how we find meaning and connection in our ordinary - or extraordinary – lives.

Recent publications from **Coverstory** *books*

Tilt - by Ian Gouge

Take four strangers arriving in London on the same train one weekday morning, then follow them as their various endeavours sees them criss-cross the capital before they take the same service north later in the day.

Will the injured sportsman be given a clean bill of health — or will he leave the capital more uncertain of his future than ever?

Will the ambitious PA be successful in her interview — or find she is unable to free herself from the shackles of her past life?

Will the repentant brother be rewarded with the forgiveness of his siblings or a longed for reacquaintance with God?

Will the egotistical playwright rise above the disappointment of a commercial 'flop' to reaffirm his course to self-anointed greatness?

Or will the City — and Life — beat them all down, four characters struggling to come to terms with the insistent demands of living?

Valley of the Kings - by Graeme Ryan (new edition)

Valley of the Kings is both excavation of family history and an incantation of voices telling contemporary stories that startle. The grieving son and the street angel; the coke addict meeting Piers Plowman in the service-station; the singing nightingale on Universal Credit; the homeless person in Ancient Egypt; the famous sax player; the young lovers in their mythic hotel: all united in 'the exquisite ache of the human day'.

Let 'the weight of the wind on tide' sing loud in this visionary debut which, in Graeme Ryan, introduces an exciting new voice to the UK poetry scene.

Once Significant Others by Ian Gouge

A group of five friends who, some thirty years after they lived and worked in the same town, come back together to honour an old friend who has recently died. The weekend is intended as a celebration but merely serves to reignite old emotions and uncover long-held secrets.

"Sally Rooney meets Henry James"

"this honest exploration of human nature helped me understand myself better"

"a story that questions the whole idea of friendship and the notion that we can ever really know anyone"

Edge and Cusp by Richard Lister

What lies beyond the familiar and tangible? In this collection Richard Lister explores what happens at life's edges. He reflects on how we respond to loss, vulnerability and hope and considers themes of perseverance and grace. Eileen Casey describes his work as 'rich in allusions and textual layers' and 'a celebration of ordinary magic perceived by a keen eye'.

Richard writes with warm empathy about people who live at the margins. These encounters are informed by his experience of living in Malawi, Cambodia and across the UK. Sky Island Journal commented that they 'rarely see this kind of emotional intimacy executed with such svelte grace'. As a semi-abstract painter, Richard writes with an artist's eye for the evocative.

An Irregular Piece of Sky - by Ian Gouge

An Irregular Piece of Sky contains fifteen contemporary stories in which we meet characters who are trying to come to terms with loss and grief, the potential of love, their histories, and the opportunities the future may offer them.

Ian Gouge introduces us to people who — just like us — are striving to make sense of their place in the world.

New Contexts: 4 by Various Authors

Once again we have been able to harvest an eclectic selection of contemporary poetry and short prose from around the world. Authors in this collection are geographically spread across the United Kingdom and the United States of America, as well as Western Europe and Australasia.

In curating these collections we are always struck how certain themes seem to emerge in each, as if the authors and poets have independently mined a contemporary theme or preoccupation.

Yet whilst there may be some commonality of theme there is, as ever, a tremendous divergence of style and approach.

Milton Keynes UK
Ingram Content Group UK Ltd.
UKHW020015290823
427665UK00013B/150